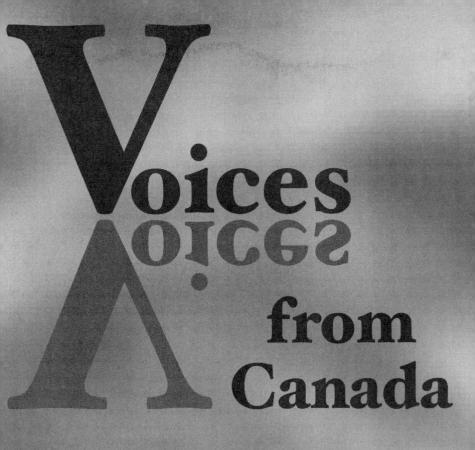

Voices

from Canada

Focus on Thirty Plays

Albert-Reiner Glaap (ed.)

Translated from the German by Nicholas Quaintmere

Voices from Canada
Focus on Thirty Plays

Albert-Reiner Glaap (ed.)

Translated from the German
by Nicholas Quaintmere

Playwrights Canada Press
Toronto • Canada

Playwrights Canada Press
54 Wolseley St., 2nd fl. Toronto, Ontario CANADA M5T 1A5
416-703-0013 fax 416-703-0059
orders@playwrightscanada.com • www.playwrightscanada.com

Playwrights Canada Press acknowledges the support of
the taxpayers of Canada and the province of Ontario through
The Canada Council for the Arts, the Government of Canada through DFAIT
and the Canadian Embassy in Germany.

The Canada Council for the Arts
Le Conseil des Arts du Canada

Department of Foreign Affairs and International Trade   Ministère des Affaires étrangères et du Commerce international

Production Editor/Cover Design: Jodi Armstrong

National Library of Canada Cataloguing in Publication

Glaap, Albert-Reiner
    Voices from Canada : focus on 30 plays / Albert-Reiner Glaap ; translated from the German by Nicholas Quaintmere.

Translation of: Stimmen aus Kanada : 25 kanadische Dramen für deutsche
    Bühnen, kanadische Dramen.
ISBN 0-88754-696-X

    1. Theatre—Canada. 2. Canadian drama—20th century. I. Quaintmere,
Nicholas P. II. Title.

PS8165.G5413 2003   792.9'5'0971   C2003-900036-2
PR9191.5.G5413 2003

First edition: February 2003.
Printed and bound by AGMV Marquis at Quebec, Canada.

—•— Table of Contents —•—

—•— Preface —•—

The original version of this book was written in German and published in Germany by Wissenschaftlicher Verlag Trier under the title *Stimmen aus Kanada: 25 kanadische Dramen für deutsche Bühnen*. Requests from some other European countries for an English translation led to this enlarged and updated version. *Voices from Canada: Focus on Thirty Plays* is intended for those readers who are interested in new trends and developments in the world of theatre. Above all it is hoped that it will be particularly useful as a handbook and reference work for dramaturgs in theatres outside Canada. One of the reasons that Canadian drama is little known outside Canada is because the independent professional theatre in Canada did not really come into existence until the seventies. Up until that point theatrical activities in this part of North America were mainly restricted to performances by regional amateur dramatic groups and productions of plays from Great Britain and the United States of America. A second reason is that the Canadian plays of the seventies and eighties were mostly of little interest to theatregoers outside of Canada. For Canadian theatre in its early phases of development was a fundamental part of the search for its own identity and its efforts to establish its cultural emancipation from the European motherlands and the USA. Regionalism and nationalism, however, have long since been replaced by globalism and multiculturalism. Canadian dramatists are now writing, like writers elsewhere, about more universal themes. The multiplicity of ethnic groups, races and immigrants living in Canada finds its expression in a literary polyphony.

This handbook is based on numerous interviews and research. It introduces the reader to 30 Canadian plays in the form of overviews. The first step in this process was to speak to dramaturges, directors and other specialists outside of Canada: what do you hope to get from Canadian plays in your theatre work? What sort of themes are interesting for you? What sort of plays would you seriously consider for production in your theatre? Which would—taking into account your knowledge of your intended audience—be out of the question?

The information that arose from this research led to the selection and reading of sixty Canadian plays which were then discussed with theatre specialists in Canada with the aim of choosing thirty plays for this book. In view of the diversity of activities in theatres across Canada, restricting the discussions to the centres of Toronto, Montréal and Vancouver would have possibly led to a very one-sided impression. There are also many very important theatres in Calgary, Edmonton, Halifax, Saskatoon, St. John's (Newfoundland) and other towns and cities. During a six-week *coast to coast* journey across Canada I spoke to theatre experts who examined the list of plays with the idea of reducing them to a "definitely" (in other words: would be suitable for performance in Europe), "definitely not" or a "maybe." Two thirds of those questioned independently recommended the same thirty plays discussed in this book. Clearly this was to no extent an "objective" choice, but its significance cannot be ignored. Three of the plays were penned by Aboriginal Canadians, six by French-Canadians and the rest by English-speaking Canadians. The plays considered for this book are all scripted ones. Performance-based plays, imagistic productions and physical theatre are not included. It would be difficult, for instance, to stage a Robert Lepage play in a European theatre without Lepage directing it. One is almost inclined to say that a Robert Lepage production needs a Robert Lepage as director.

In the *Introduction*, which follows this *Preface*, Jerry Wasserman examines the chosen works and presents his valuable insight on the situation in Canada, for which I would like to offer my thanks here. Wasserman is a professor at the University of British Columbia in Vancouver: he has made great contributions to Canadian drama both as a stage director and, above all, with his edition of the two-volume anthology *Modern Canadian Plays* (Vancouver: Talonbooks 1993-94).

It is hoped that *Voices from Canada* will, via its concise information and comments, give its readers an overview of some of the most important plays of recent years and thereby an insight into contemporary Canadian theatre. Interested theatres will be able to decide whether they would like to perform one of the plays and, of course, which one. The 30 plays are presented in alphabetic order (of their respective authors) and all according to the same pattern. Specific details regarding first performance, director, cast of characters, stage setting, information regarding available editions, as well as information about performance rights and the author's agents are followed by a summary of the content of the plays. This is followed by a section entitled "Background and Commentary" which provides information about the context of the play and the author and his work as well as tips about potential performances of the play (where possible). This is rounded off with useful lists of keywords, central themes and some other plays by the respective authors.

This central core of the book is followed by a list of further noteworthy Canadian plays and the essay "After Words" written especially for this book by Robert Wallace, professor at York University in Toronto who concentrates on forms of performance which are not included in this handbook but "flourish equally well across Canada."

At the end of the book you will find short explanations concerning the Playwrights Guild of Canada (PGC) and Le Centre des Auteurs Dramatiques (CEAD), the two most important centres of information for English-Canadian and French-Canadian drama in Canada, and an index of plays which have been nominated or have won the Governor General's Literary Award. Finally, there is a short bibliography of anthologies of

Canadian plays and works of secondary literature.

Voices From Canada was put together particularly for European countries in which English rather than German is spoken. Only a few Canadian plays have so far been staged in European theatres. The plays considered do not amount to anything like a canon; other and different plays could have been taken into consideration. It was, however, important to select plays that do not require detailed knowledge about the context the particular play stems from. Also, the plays should not present grave linguistic barriers, considering the fact that in most European countries they would be staged in translated versions.

Finally, I have the not onerous task of mentioning those people who have worked with me on this book. I would like to thank my interview partners in Canada for their openness and their invaluable information; the authors of the plays and their agents for their support; Jerry Wasserman and Bob Wallace for their knowledgeable contributions which underpin the structure of this book, and Yvette Nolan for her contribution on the Playwrights Guild. Without the information and material provided by the Playwrights Guild of Canada in Toronto and CEAD in Montréal it would hardly have been possible to complete this book; my particular thanks go to Angela Rebeiro, Tony Hamill, Michael Petrasek and Linda Gaboriau. Further thanks must go to those who have helped create this book, namely Susann Damati and Elke Müller-Scheck.

I would particularly like to thank Nicholas Quaintmere for his translation and revisions to the text and Michael Heinze for providing very useful material to this publication. I owe my wife a huge thank you for supporting my great love of the theatre and all my activities in that regard, as well as her critical help and the time she has given me for the realisation of this project.

Albert-Reiner Glaap

—•— Introduction —•—

Getting a fix on Canadian theatre in the late 1990s is more difficult than it was in the 1970s, when attempts to answer Northrop Frye's question "Where is here?" focused largely on issues of Canadian content: history, regional geography, social conflicts. Where is here now, two decades later? With nationalism gone out of fashion for the moment in favour of globalism, with cultural self-consciousness challenged by the post structuralist elimination of the self, the borders that once defined "here" have blurred. The frontiers of Canada are *fronteras americanas*. *Toronto, Mississippi* no longer seems so absurd an address. "Canada," we acknowledge, is only one of many possible worlds, as open to construction, negotiation, and redefinition by playwrights as by politicians. When new Canadian kids are as likely to speak Mandarin as English or French, as likely to relate to Harlem as to Hogtown, who "we" are exactly becomes more and more problematic. In reflecting these various changes, demographic and otherwise, Canadian theatre has become an increasingly heterogeneous place. Obviously, no selection of plays can claim to be fully representative of a national repertoire or, in the case of Quebec and what has come to be known as "The Rest of Canada," a bi-national repertoire; or, considering the various Canadian First Nations, a multinational repertoire. But what Albert-Reiner Glaap has managed to do in his handbook is showcase the broad range of Canadian dramatic subjects and strategies available to producers, directors, actors and teachers in 30 modern plays of acute theatrical interest.

Two of the earliest, *Billy Bishop Goes to War* and *Jitters*, hearken back to the era of nationalist self-examination when Canadian attempts to excel always seemed entangled in identity crises directly attributable to the monolithic imperialism of Britain and the United States. Both John Gray and David French, take a comic, metatheatrical approach to these anxieties, their dramatic personae speaking in the traditional Canadian voice of self-deprecating irony. We hear that voice again in Guillermo Verdecchia's *Fronteras Americanas*, but with a different political accent. Whereas the earlier plays enact a binary colonial model, the 1990s perspective of *Fronteras Americanas* sees identity, personal and national, as a matrix of fluid cultural and historical forces in continual negotiation. Verdecchia's play also rings variations on the monologue form used so successfully in *Billy Bishop Goes to War*. Another instance of that form, Daniel MacIvor's *House*, abjures politics for an examination of personal and theatrical boundaries. Incorporating elements of stand-up comedy and performance art, *House* is by turns harrowing and hilarious, an interior journey edged with existential despair.

The urban sophistication of MacIvor's dramatic world differs greatly from the stereotypical image of a Canadian literature and theatre concerned primarily with rural, agrarian or savage wilderness landscapes. In a Canada that has become overwhelmingly urbanised, playwrights often find their most savage landscapes in the wilderness of the city, and in the hearts of those who live there. Edmonton, Toronto and Montreal are the sites of murders in works by three of contemporary Canada's most acclaimed playwrights, Brad Fraser's *Unidentified Human Remains and the True Nature of Love,* Judith Thompson's *Lion in the Streets* and René-Daniel Dubois' *Being at Home with Claude.* Violence in each play is closely intertwined with the confusions of love and sex, straight and gay, along with other permutations of alienated life in the modern metropolis. As an expression of personal alienation, the monologue form looms large in these plays, as it does in Morris Panych's *7 Stories,* a comic treatment of the multivocal meta-narratives from which the tapestry of contemporary city living is woven.

Canadian playwrights today continue to explore the way families shape, or misshape, the individual. But unlike the familiar oedipal drama with its primary father-son conflict, the new plays often focus on female experience and the dramatic roles of mother, daughter and sister. Joan MacLeod's *Toronto, Mississippi,* Marie Laberge's *Aurélie, ma sœur* and Drew Hayden Taylor's *Someday* each offer a unique distillation of the mother-daughter relationship. One daughter is mentally handicapped, another a child of incest, the third seized from her Native mother at infancy and raised white. All three plays largely avoid the temptations of melodrama in favour of the bittersweet complexity and irresolution of real life. In contrast to their theatrical realism, Sharon Pollock's *Doc* employs the subjectivities of memory and the divided self as a daughter revisits the scene of her mother's death and figuratively puts her father—and herself—on trial for murder.

Michel Tremblay examines the split female subject in an even more radical form in *Albertine, in Five Times,* a synchronic view of one woman at war with herself over five different decades of her life. Tremblay's title character is at once mother, daughter and sister, a poignant portrait of the *Québécoise* by Canada's most popular and successful playwright. Rural Québec provides the setting for Michel Marc Bouchard's *The Orphan Muses,* in which three sisters and a brother engage in battles of the imagination to commemorate their missing mother. Family provides more of a backdrop than a formal setting for the darkly comic life and loves of Sally Clark's heroine in *Moo,* and for the sexual and spiritual travails of Raymond Storey's characters in his funny and profound play about AIDS, *The Saints and Apostles,* a Canadian variation on *Angels in America.*

Family and religion create a volatile mix in two very different dramatic treatments of abuse focusing on women. Connie Gault's prairie gothic *Sky* spins an oddly fascinating story of incest, while in *Sisters* Wendy Lill turns the lens of memory on the nuns who carried out the destructive policies of their surrogate family, the church, towards Native children in a residential school. Characteristic of current Canadian theatrical practice, both plays avoid a sociological or documentary approach to social problems. Similarly, in launching the current movement of Native playwriting in Canada, Tomson Highway's *The Rez Sisters* subordinates the social ills of an extended family of seven unforgettable women to a rich comic celebration of their humanity, with dirge notes mostly in a minor key. In addition to Highway and Drew Hayden Taylor, Daniel David Moses illustrates the range of contemporary Native writing in his post-modern, burlesque retelling of a violent episode from Canada's sorry history, of Native-white relations, *Almighty Voice*. Like Moses, but for different reasons, John Murrell plays with stereotypical images of frontier history in his study of romantic passion in the Canadian West, *Farther West*.

As a popular subject of post-colonial revisionism, Shakespeare and his age appear in these plays in a broad variety of ways. Normand Chaurette's *The Queens* presents the intrigues of six female monarchs in the court of Richard III in the imagistic style characteristic of so much Québécois dramatic writing today. In a very different vein, Ann-Marie MacDonald re-presents Shakespearean fictional history as feminist metafictional "herstory." *Goodnight Desdemona (Good Morning Juliet)* combines blank verse, metatheatrics and cross-dressing with a pinch of alchemy and Jung in a hilarious rewriting of *Othello* and *Romeo and Juliet*. *Othello* also provides the paradigm for what Djanet Sears calls her "rhapsodic blues tragedy," *Harlem Duet*. This fascinating examination of Black female identity and interracial marriage seen from a Black woman's point of view depicts variations on the relationship between Othello and his pre-Desdemona Black wife during slave times, the Harlem Renaissance and the present day.

Even with so much investment in the stories of those who traditionally have suffered theatrical marginalization—women, gays, Aboriginal Canadians, people of colour—the stories of straight white men in (and out of) power are seen here in four plays ranging widely in styles and approaches. An ad agency transforms into a bunker in *Warriors*, Michel Garneau's paradoxically poetic look at the commodification of militarism. George F. Walker constructs a Nietzschean comedy of mock-metaphysics out of the exploits of his anachronistic master criminal in *Zastrozzi* (the earliest of all these plays, dating from 1977). Jason Sherman's *Patience* raises somewhat more serious metaphysical and ethical questions in dramatising the Job-like tale of a nasty man whose sudden loss of everything he thinks he holds dear invites us to reassess the meaning of life. And John Mighton crosses George Walker with Tom Stoppard, marrying speculative science and *film noir* in the deadpan murder mystery *Possible Worlds*.

Finally, two fine plays represent the sophistication of Canadian theatre for young audiences, a genre that has been particularly strong in both French and English over the past two decades. The young people in Suzanne Lebeau's *Les Petits Pouvoirs* fight for their independence in the face of well-meaning parental interference, while in Dennis Foon's innovative international success, *New Canadian Kid*, they struggle to cope with the stresses of adjusting to a new language and culture.

Canada has long been a net exporter of raw materials and an importer of culture. In recent years the balance of trade has begun to shift, if only subtly, as Canadian novelists, film actors and pop stars become international celebrities. Though no Canadian playwright has yet achieved the stature of a Margaret Atwood or Céline Dion, more and more of the plays originating on Canadian stages are finding a wider audience. As Canadian theatre continues to track the evolving nature of who we are and where "here" is—how we live together in the sometimes frustrating and often bewildering complexity of what Guillermo Verdecchia calls "this Noah's Ark of a nation"—the fascinating plays that speak with a fresh voice to ourselves of ourselves will find their way more frequently onto the world stage. This handbook should provide a useful guide to theatres and theatre people, both in Canada and abroad, who want to sample those voices, to hear what some of us new kids have to say.

Jerry Wasserman
Department of English
University of British Columbia

Thirty Voices From Canada

The Orphan Muses

Michel Marc Bouchard

Premiere (Fr.): 1989, *Théâtre d'Aujourd'hui*, Montréal, Québec;
Premiere (Eng.): commissioned by *Banff Playwrights' Colony* and first produced in 1993, *Ubu Repertory Theater*, New York
Director: Jackie Maxwell
Cast: 1 man, 3 women
Stage Setting: Saint-Ludger de Milot, in the Lac-Saint-Jean region of Québec
Publisher/Place/Year: (Fr.) Leméac Éditeur 1989; (Eng.) Scirocco, Winnipeg, Manitoba 1995
Running time: 1 hour 30
Performance rights: Des Landes, Dickinson et associés, 4171 Hampton Avenue, Montréal, Québec H4A 2L1

Characters
CATHERINE
ISABELLE
LUC
MARTINE

Summary
20th January, 1944: A stranger moves into the house, where Lucien and Jacqueline Tangay are living with their four children, a lonely house in Saint-Ludger de Milot, Canada. The stranger, Frederico Rosa, is one of the

workers building a dam on River Peribonka. He is Spanish, and Jacqueline buys a Spanish dictionary by mail order. "Those who learn the language of the foreigner, give their soul to Satan," the vicar preaches.

The scandal spreads quickly in the small village. People talk about the family because of the love between Lucien's wife and the stranger – they talk, even before Jacqueline leaves her husband and family to follow Frederico to Spain. Lucien joins the army and is killed in battle in Normandy. His comrades called him the "suicide." In order not to distress the youngest daughter, Isabelle, the three other children tell her that her mother is dead.

Now, Isabelle is 27 and living with her eldest sister Catherine who has brought her up *in lieu* of the mother. She is said to be "mentally deprived." Martine has followed in her father's footsteps and joined the army. She is stationed at Baden-Solingen. Luc, the only brother, is writing a book: *Letters of a Spanish Queen to her Son.*

Over the years, all the children have tried to cope with their past in their own ways; they have tried to forget, to cope by writing about it or even to believe in the tale of the mother being dead.

On Easter 1965 all children meet up again for the first time in a very long time at the house they grew up in. Isabelle has brought them together under different pretences. And she has got a special surprise for all of them: Mama is coming back.

Background and commentary

The Orphan Muses has been described by some reviewers as a deeply disturbing play, possibly because it not only shows the disrupted left-over members of a particular family but also because it tells a fundamental truth about the concept of "family" as such: families often have a habit of burying their problems. All the members of this family are trying to cope with what happened to their parents; they are trying to define their own identity. They are not sure what roles to play in a family that can only marginally be called thus. Having lost their "models" they try to be "Mom" and "Dad" themselves, and they are unsure when to tell the truth and when to hide behind their self-constructed identities.

It is probably Bouchard's greatest achievement that the play does not sink into gloom and a general feeling of doomed existence but keeps a touch of light humour that sets the audience free to think about the questions the author raises. This is his aim: to ask questions rather than answer them.

This examination of family, abandonment and identity is one of more than 20 plays Michel Marc Bouchard has written since getting his BA in Theatre Studies in 1980. His work has been highly acclaimed and won several prizes. So far, his plays have been translated into nine languages and performed on four continents.

In several of his plays the exploration of homosexuality plays a vital role, but in *The Orphan Muses* it is only a subtle undertone. The character of Martine certainly does not hide her sexuality but if the character is presented in too butch a way she runs the risk of gliding into a stereotype. The same applies to Luc: his cross-dressing is a desperate attempt to bring back a bit of his mother rather than an expression of his sexuality. "Bouchard is concerned that the most obviously eccentric character, Luc, not be presented as a drag queen. 'I don't even know if Luc is gay or not,' he insists. 'For me, wearing his mother's dress is more of a political statement against the village. Martine, she's gay and she's proud of it. But Luc – I think he has more problems than thinking about if he's gay or not.'" (Colin Thomas. "Aftershocks of a Family Collapse." *The Georgia Straight*, March 7-14, 1996.) This makes the role so difficult to play: the character must be portrayed as sincere and dignified and should not verge on the ridiculous or stereotypical.

Another character to be explored carefully is Isabelle. She might be considered an imbecile in the beginning but later on she appears to be the one responsible for the denouement. In contrast to what she seems to be in Act I, she is now like the classical "idiot savante," not an off-stage character. In the end she plays a significant role.

Themes
• The concept of family
• Abandonment and identity
• Probing the secrets of a past

Some other plays
• *Les Grandes Chaleurs* (Leméac Éditeur)
  Heat Wave – translated by Bill Glassco (Scirocco Drama, Winnipeg)
• *Le Voyage du Couronnement* (Leméac Éditeur)
  The Coronation Voyage – translated by Linda Gaboriau (CEAD and Factory Theatre, Toronto)
• *L'Histoire de l'oie* (Leméac Éditeur)
  The Tale of Teeka – translated by Linda Gaboriau (Talonbooks, Vancouver)
• *Le Chemin des Passes-Dangereuses* (Leméac Éditeur)
  Dangerous Passes Road – translated by Linda Gaboriau (Talonbooks, Vancouver)

The Queens/
Les Reines

Normand
Chaurette

Premiere (Fr.): 18th January 1991, *Théâtre d'Aujourd'hui*, Montréal, Québec
Director: André Brassard
Premiere (Eng.): 6th November 1992, *Canadian Stage Company,* Toronto, Ontario
Director: Peter Hinton
Cast: 6 women
Stage Setting: Royal Palace in London; 1483
Publisher/Place/Year: (Fr.) Leméac/Actes Sud-Papiers, Paris 1991; (Eng.) Coach House Press, Toronto, Ontario 1992
Running Time: 2 hours
Performance rights: J.C. Goodwin et Associates, 839 est, rue Sherbrooke, Suite 2, Montréal, Québec H2L 1K6, 514-598-5252, fax 514-598-1878

Characters
ANNE DEXTER: Sister of Edward, George and Richard
ANNE WARWICK: future Queen of England
ISABEL WARWICK: her sister, George's wife
QUEEN MARGARET: earlier Queen of England
QUEEN ELIZABETH: Queen of England, Edward's wife
DUCHESS OF YORK: mother of Anne Dexter, Edward, George and Richard

Summary

London, January 1483. In an atmosphere of horror and cruelty five women fight for power in England.

The Duchess of York is the mother of Anne Dexter, Edward, George and Richard, but she does not acknowledge Anne as her daughter. She hangs her affection on her retarded son George who is also dumb. Edward, the reigning monarch, lies on his deathbed and is to be replaced by Richard—shortly to be married to Lady Anne Warwick—provided that George and the children of the Regent have been "disposed of."

Queen Elizabeth, Edward's wife, lives in constant fear of losing her power and all the privileges which go with it. She reacts to the news of her husband's death by lapsing into a state of mental confusion.

Queen Margaret, the previous queen of England, has been forced by "Yorkists" to abdicate. Deeply embittered she attempts to turn her back on London, the city she hates. She cannot, however, break away for good and keeps returning.

Anne Warwick only accepts a marriage proposal from the cripple, Richard, in order to gain the throne. Her ambition outweighs even her fear of the position.

The cynical Isabel Warwick, her sister, is married to George, a marriage which also arose purely from a striving for power. Isabel is shocked when she establishes that her husband is by no means dumb, rather that he remains silent out of solidarity with his disowned sister. When George is finally murdered by Richard, Isabel is forced to give up all her aspirations to the throne.

Anne Dexter is the only one of the six main characters who is not obsessed with thoughts of fame and the throne. She speaks only in the presence of the Duchess of York; otherwise she refuses to say anything. Her mother has had both her hands amputated and disowned her. Up to this point she had had a very close relationship with her brother George.

When Edward's death is finally confirmed, Anne Warwick proclaims herself queen of England, although Elizabeth's children—despite all rumours to the contrary—are still alive. However before she assumes the throne she allows the Duchess of York to wear the crown for ten seconds. Having fulfilled her lifetime's dream, albeit for only a very short time, the Duchess is able to die content.

Background and Commentary

Of the English version of *Les Reines* (translated by Linda Gaboriau) Peter Hinton, the director of its premiere on the 6th November 1992 in Toronto, wrote:

> *The Queens* is much more than a re-examination of Shakespeare's *Richard III*, or a backstage pastiche on the goings-on in 1483. It's a reworking of history: Shakespeare's queens in a dream of themselves, an imagining of our

world through the glass of time. It captures those brilliant flashes of truth just as everything falls. Like dreams the text plays with our mythology and assumptions and gives substantial credence to the imagination in the face of justice. Are the babies alive or dead? Is Anne Dexter real? How did she lose her hands? Why is George sequestered in the storage cellars? All these questions which are unanswerable, yet full of many possibilities – all are part of the mystery.

At the end of this foreword Hinton turns to the potential audience and tells them: in all this mystery avoid the temptation to work at its meaning. Let the play work on you, lovely stranger; its rewards are life-changing.

In *Les Reines* Normand Chaurette investigates the passions and the ambition of six women from Shakespeare's historical dramas. The emotional and politically determined search for validity is timeless and common to them all. The critic Wladimir Krysinski wrote in the theatre journal *Jey*: "The representation of the conversations of the queens as well the way they take place behind closed doors is certainly a master-stroke." And he continues:

> This is the negative side of royal power, which is traditionally reserved for men. Chaurette's dialogue [...] is aimed at making the confusion of feelings and bad moods visible; the conflicts that do not even exist any more, the memories which, however, still cause pain.... These queens seem to be wax-works which are only rarely, if at all, seen.

The text of *Les Reines* is poetic. It sends the reader on a quest that never reaches a definitive end. Every time one feels one has reached the end of the search one finds oneself back at the beginning again. Therein lies the charm of the play. The mysteriousness unfolds during many-sided passages of text and expresses itself more and more through simple connections.

The original production, directed by André Brassard was praised in the press for both its dramatic originality and the sensitivity and creativity with which Brassard handled the text. As Robert Lévesque wrote at the time in *Le Devoir*:

> Il y a dans le texte des *Reines* milles nuances que la mise en scène de Brassard engouffre dans un maelstrom de sens où ne surnagent que les réflexes-clichés dramatiques, la colère ouverte, le satire féroce, la séduction hypocrite, le cri vengeur, le rire démoniaque, les chocs de niveaux de langage, etc., réflexes derrière ou sous lesquels Chaurette place ses effets plus essentiels, son théâtre. (*Le Devoir*, 24ᵗʰ January 1991)

Les Reines is a piece for actresses which challenges their creativity. It was performed in various Canadian theatres and in New York, Florence, Brussels and Paris. Between 1973 and 1983 the author, born in Montréal in 1954, wrote 65 pieces for Radio Canada and for the theatre journal *Jey*.

Later he was the head of one of the large publishing houses in Québec (Leméac Éditeur) for five years. Chaurette is the author of six stage-plays. In the eighties Chaurette, together with Daniel Bouchard, gave theatre in Québec a new direction which reflected common themes such as creation, death and madness and therefore led theatre away from its previously nationalistic tendencies.

At this point it is worth drawing attention to the contribution of the translator, Linda Gaboriau. Born in Boston, she studied at McGill University in Montréal and then produced and presented numerous radio programs on CBC and Radio Canada as well as writing reviews for the *Gazette* (Montréal). In the meantime she has translated more than 30 stage plays from French into English including works by some of the best-known dramatists in Québec.

Themes
• Ambition, striving for power
• Dreams and passions
• Power structures in court
• Private, familial conflicts and rivalries.
• The traditional and modern understanding of the roles of men and women

Some other plays
• *Je vous écris du Caire* (Leméac Éditeur)
  All the Verdis of Venice – translated by Linda Gaboriau
• *Fragments d'une lettre d'adieu lus par des géologues* (Leméac Éditeur)
  Fragments of a Farewell Letter Read by Geologists – translated by Linda Gaboriau (Talonbooks, Vancouver)

Moo

Sally Clark

Premiere: 1988, *Nova Playwrights '88,* co-production with the *Alberta Theatre Projects,* Calgary, Alberta and *The Belfry Theatre,* Victoria, British Columbia

Director: Glynis Leyshon

Cast: 17 (10 women, 7 men); can be played with 8 actors (5 women, 3 men)

Stage Setting: Various locations including a mental hospital, a hotel room, front of a house, bedroom/living room, a tropical paradise

Publisher/Place/Year: Playwrights Canada Press, Toronto, Ontario 1984

Length: 132 pages

Performance rights: Shain Jaffe, Great North Artists, 350 Dupont Street, Toronto, Ontario M5R 1V9, 416-925-2051, fax 416-925-3904

Characters

MORAGH MACDOWELL: Moo
HARRY PARKER: Moo's husband
SARAH MACDOWELL: Moo's eldest sister
DITTY MACDOWELL: Moo's sister
MR. MACDOWELL: Moo's father
MRS. MACDOWELL: Moo's mother
MAUDE GORMLEY: Harry's second wife
NURSE/RECEPTIONIST
DOCTOR

Summary

Moo tells the unconventional, passionate story of the love affair of Moo McDowell and the "rotter" Harry Parker. "Rotters" are those who seduce well-to-do women and then leave them, thereby ruining their lives. In numerous reminiscences and monologues by the individual characters the viewer slowly experiences how Moo marries Harry, how he has her admitted to psychotherapy and then goes on to marry two more times. Harry regularly sends Moo postcards from his travels in far off lands which always leads to Moo travelling after him – always without success.

Moo's family warns her against continuing to trail after Harry, but even at 65 years of age she doesn't give up. She is so obsessed with the desire to bind Harry to her that while searching for him she completely neglects her family and her own son, whom she eventually loses.

However, Harry is also unable to forget Moo and his actions are indirectly determined by her.

Years later, when he meets her by chance in a hospital, he decides to make a clean break. He returns alone during the night and shoots her.

Background and Commentary

Moo was first performed in 1988. The title figure is based on one of the author's rather talkative aunts, although the play is by no means autobiographical. The name "Moo" is a short form of Moragh.

Sally Clark began her working life as a painter and then began attending courses in playwriting at York University. Today she says of herself: "I do paintings for peace; I write plays for excitement." *Jehanne of the Witches* (1989), a reworking of the Jean d'Arc myth, *The Trial of Judith K.* (1989), an adaptation of Kafka's *Der Prozess*, and *Life Without Instruction* (1991) are her best known works for the stage.

The playwright explained, with reference to *Moo*, that she is particularly interested in the comparison between young and old. She wanted, in this play, to encompass somebody's entire life: what would happen between the two poles of youth and old age? How does ageing change a person? The author takes her audience with her on a journey – temporally and spatially: from 1912 to 1972, forwards and backwards, from Vancouver to Seattle and to the paradise regions of the tropics. The central figures are Moo and —as one might say these days—one of the "co-stars" of this chapter of her life, Harry Parker. The two characters act as representatives of different philosophies of life. Moo wants to use and enjoy her life to the full with all the strength at her disposal. When she sees Harry for the first time she knows that nothing and no one will stop her from making herself his. But Harry, on the other hand, is a rotter, one of that unpleasant type of men who ruin women (particularly rich women), as Sally Clark's grandmother told her with reference to various cases. When, at the beginning of the play, Harry shoots at Moo and then has her admitted to a psychiatric clinic claiming to be her brother (and not her husband); when he then disappears, sends her postcards from little known tropical islands and weds two other women, then the viewer asks himself or herself: what is it that Moo finds so great about Harry that causes her, after her release from the clinic, to search for him all over the globe? What is the root of her obsession?

Obsession is the *leitmotif* in *Moo*, or to be more specific the inexplicable affection that one person can feel for another, irrespective of their shortcomings. Harry has great respect for Moo's tenacity although (or perhaps even because) she pursues him. Despite everything, Moo finds herself once more embroiled in a love affair with him. She knows that she will achieve nothing with her pursuit of Harry, but she continues nevertheless. Her resolve is much greater than Harry could ever have suspected. She is completely and utterly in love with a man who is no good for her yet whose actions at the end of the day are determined by her.

Moo is a play about a dysfunctional relationship, a tragic romance which in its own part triggers comical actions and dialogue at times. *Dark comedy, bizarre characters, funny, sad, satirical* – these are all words which repeatedly appear in reviews of the play in Canada. In the words of Cecily M. Barrie in the *Canadian Book Review* 1991, 242:

> It is the sound and imagery of violence that darken Moo's story. Several times throughout the play, Clark jolts the audience with a man unexpectedly shooting a woman. And Moo expresses her final regrets in bitter terms: "Whenever I see one of those [Chinese watercolour] paintings, with that tiny little bird sitting on a branch, do you know what I want to do?... Blast its little brains out!"

Sally Clark said herself, in an interview with the critic Jon Kaplan in January 1989, that she was at first distraught when a reading of certain scenes from *Moo* occasionally provoked laughter from the audience. But then it became clear to her how a comedy ought to be written: "If you write to be funny, it usually won't work – simply creating jokes doesn't make a play into a comedy. A real comedy has to be written with some seriousness."

Indeed Clark's play oscillates between comedy and tragedy. Occasionally one is reminded of Joe Orton or even Alan Ayckbourn.

Seventeen characters appear in this play – ten women and seven men. Eight actors (five women, three men) are, however, enough to make up the complement. The characters around Moo and Harry—Moo's sisters and parents, Harry's second and third wives, doctors and nurses etc.—reflect facets of a society to which Moo isn't suited at all. The role of Moo presents a great challenge to any actress: she must be able to play Moo convincingly as both a young and an old woman.

Themes

- Unconventional relationships
- The problems of growing old
- Inner "journeys" and real journeys
- Different philosophies of life
- Love versus rejection

Some other plays

Available from Playwrights Guild of Canada:
- *Lost Souls and Missing Persons* (in *Dangerous Traditions*)
- *Ten Ways to Abuse an Old Woman* (in *Playing the Pacific Province: An Anthology of British Columbia Plays 1967 - 2000*)
- *Trial of a Ladies Man* (in *Rhubarb-o-rama*)

Available from Talonbooks:
- *Jehanne of the Witches*
- *Life without Instruction*
- *Saint Frances of Hollywood*
- *Trial of Judith K.*
- *Wasps*

Being at Home with Claude

René-Daniel Dubois

Premiere (Fr.): 13th November 1985, *Théâtre de Quat'sous*, Montréal, Québec

Director: Daniel Roussel

Premiere (Eng.): 7th April 1987, *Tarragon Theatre*, Toronto, Ontario

Director: Duncan McIntosh

Cast: 4 men

Stage Setting: Judge's office in the Palais de Justice in Montréal, Québec; July 1967

Publisher/Place/Year: (Fr.) Leméac; Ottawa, Ontario 1986; (Eng.) *Canadian Theatre Review* 50/Spring 1987

Running Time: 1 hour 40

Performance rights: J. C. Goodwin et Associates, 839 est, rue Sherbrooke, Suite 2, Montréal, Québec H2L IK6, 514-598-5252, fax 514-598-1878

Characters

LUI (YVES): early twenties, thin, nervous

L'INSPECTEUR (ROBERT): late thirties

LE STÉNOGRAPHE (GUY): assistant to the inspector; same age as his boss; heavy smoker

LE POLICIER (LATREILLE): member of the security services in the Palais de Justice, has no idea what is going on in the judge's office and couldn't care less.

Summary

The play is set in the office of Judge Delorme in the Palais de Justice in Montréal at the time of the World Exposition in 1967. A young man (Lui) is being repeatedly interrogated by a police inspector (Robert). The action takes place in the hour preceding the expected arrival of the judge. The young man, Yves, has killed—as it turns out—Claude, a man who moves in the "better circles," and has given himself up to the police two days later. The inspector is already aware of the circumstances of the murder but is clueless as to the motive. Another confusing fact is that Yves has the key to Judge Delorme's office. He refuses to leave the office before he has spoken to the judge.

During the course of Yves' rudimentary statements it becomes slowly clear to the audience how the deed was committed. After committing the murder he has asked the inspector and a reporter to come and meet him at the judge's office. The scandal arises, of all times, just at the time of the Expo – when the city is full of tourists and any commotion about violent crime is to be avoided. Later, the inspector determines Yves' identity: Yves has a sister, lives in a slum and works as a rent-boy on Dominion Square. The autopsy on Claude's body reveals that he has been killed during a voluntary sex act with another man. Claude has kept an encoded diary in which he has written exclusively about Yves for the last month. Claude was twenty-two, a literature student, living alone, a separatist; he had lived in Montréal for two years. Yves is astonished when an alleged girlfriend is mentioned in the diary.

The investigator is in a dilemma. In order to avoid any scandal during Expo he has been instructed to release no details to the press. However, the reporter that Yves requested is waiting outside. Then the murder victim's girlfriend arrives who denies any homosexual tendencies on the part of her boyfriend, and finally his parents who want everything hushed up. In addition to all these people, there is Yves whose story is not at all conclusive. Gradually the inspector and Yves develop a sort of mutual trust. After the inspector has sent the reporter away he prepares everything for the arrival of the judge. Yves is finally ready to talk and holds a long monologue. He was seriously in love with Claude who returned his feelings and was even prepared to accept his work on Dominion Square. For the first time Yves felt understood and respected. Despite their superficial differences the two had felt that they were kindred spirits. Their mutual love was of such an intensity that Yves, in the middle of making love, at the point of their simultaneous orgasms and possessed by such a feeling of complete bodily and intellectual unity, had taken a knife that just happened to be lying there and cut Claude's throat – to protect him from the evils of the world. Yves had wanted Claude to die at a moment of extreme happiness. Murder because of love.

It is not clear whether Judge Delorme—as the text implies—really is one of Yves' customers and the sort who, after the sexual act, are so ashamed of themselves that they treat the rent-boy like dirt. If the Judge actually is one of Yves' punters then that would perhaps explain how his key came into Yves' possession.

When the judge arrives Yves throws the key onto his table and leaves the office through a side door without saying a word. His fate and that of the judge remain a mystery.

Background and Commentary

At the beginning of this play the audience becomes witness to an interrogation that has already been going on for some hours. What has happened becomes quickly apparent. Yet the inspector is unable to tease out of Yves his motive for the crime. The inspector is furious and the interrogation stretches out over the course of the whole play; ninety minutes of oppressive intensity and electric tension. The fragmentary statements that one hears from Yves are a stark contrast to the wearing eloquence that he unloads onto the audience in his 37-minute-long monologue at the end of the play. Between these two poles the two men's physical and psychological confrontation creates a confusion of dramatic tension. The other characters succeed only infrequently to interrupt the stifling tension. The inspector, who at the beginning is only aware of his duty, proves during the course of the play to be an active force. It is his sympathy and understanding that provoke the monologue in which Yves precisely reconstructs the events of the fatal night. He tries to find the right words to express the feelings that overcame him as Claude welcomed him into his flat and prepared the dinner. For the first time he had felt "at home;" for the first time in his life he felt love. Yves increasingly recognises the truth as he attempts to formulate his recollections about his horrendous deeds in the right words. Slowly, despite the gruesome events of two nights previously, the audience find themselves slowly beginning to empathise with the killer.

Being at Home with Claude is a journey into the dark areas of the human soul, into the tangle of passions that lurk beneath the surface in every person in the modern world. It is a play which vividly—and occasionally with brutal openness—exposes the homosexual underworld. As Jaie LaPlante described it in the *St. Albert Gazette* (on 16th March 1988):

> [...]it is very much a gay play, and it is not easy to watch – especially with such graphic descriptions of the sordid details of the grisly sexual slaying. But what's more powerful about this play is in the sub-contexts of little man versus bureaucratic authority, victim vs. criminal, failed artist vs. apathetic society – larger themes that will stir angry responses in anyone who braves the emotionally brutal experience of *Being at Home with Claude*.

René-Daniel Dubois chose the year 1967 as the temporal setting for his play, the year of Expo, the world exhibition which took place in Montréal on the occasion of Canada's centenary and which attracted huge numbers of tourists. The rebellion of the separatist movement at that time raises *Being at Home with Claude* above the representation of complex personal relationships and lends the play an historical dimension.

The play, which received its French-speaking premiere in Montréal, was premiered in English (in a translation by Linda Gaboriau) at the Tarragon Theatre in Toronto in April 1987.

René-Daniel Dubois is one of the most important writers of French-speaking Québec.

Themes
- Making homosexuality a taboo issue
- Guilt and responsibility
- Understanding versus judgement
- From confrontation to communication

Some other plays
- *Le printemps, monsieur Deslauriers* (Guérin litterature)
  It's springtime, Mr. Deslauriers! – translated by Linda Gaboriau (Translation commissioned by Theatre Plus, Toronto)
- Et *Laura ne réspondait rien* (Leméac Éditeur)
  But Laura didn't answer... – translated by Linda Gaboriau (first produced by CBC Radio)

New Canadian Kid

Dennis Foon

Premiere: September 1981, *Green Thumb Theatre for Young People*, Vancouver, British Columbia, and *Calgary International Festival for Young People*, Calgary, Alberta
Director: Jane Howard Baker
Cast: 4 (1 woman, 1 girl, 2 boys)
Stage Setting: Various locations including a classroom, a playground, a house and a verandah
Publisher/Place/Year: Pulp Press, Vancouver, British Columbia 1989
Length: 45 pages
Performance rights: Peter Zednik, Green Thumb Theatre, 1885 Venables, Vancouver, British Columbia V5L 2H6, 604-254-4055, fax 604-251-7002

Characters
MOTHER: a woman from "Homeland"
NICK: her son
MENCH: a Canadian girl
MUG: a Canadian boy

Summary
Nick turns to the audience and explains that he and his mother have just emigrated to Canada. They lived previously in the fictitious country "Homeland." He has had to leave his friends behind and learn a new

language which is totally strange to him: English. In his new school Nick meets two Canadian children Mench and Mug, whose conversations he is unable to follow. Because of this language barrier, and also because of his strange style of dress, Nick is teased so much that he runs home from school before the lessons are over. In time, however, he makes friends with Mench who—in contrast to Mug—is ready to help him integrate into his new neighbourhood and to teach him a little of the language. Nick's mother also has difficulties finding her feet in her new home: after doing her shopping at the supermarket she is shouted at by Canadians who angrily point at her seemingly for no reason.

During the course of the play Nick begins to be accepted not only by Mench but also by others of his fellow pupils. He gradually begins to feel at home in Canada.

Background and Commentary

On a specifically Canadian level *New Canadian Kid* deals with the problems and in particular the isolation of immigrants who have just arrived in Canada, who must accustom themselves to Canadian culture and often only speak a little English. On a general level the problems of racism, tolerance and multiculturalism are thematized. The play, which was developed in a workshop at the Lord Roberts School in Vancouver, received its first public performance in 1981. "The children, most immigrants themselves, interviewed other New Canadians who spoke about their own experiences," wrote Foon in the introduction to the published edition of *New Canadian Kid*. "The resulting transcripts were then edited by the children, and a script, *Immigrant Children Speak*, was developed. The script was then performed by the drama club in the school." The idea of having the Canadian children in this play speak a barely understandable argot and the immigrants speak English came from the director Jane Howard Baker.

It is Foon's intention to make clear to theatregoers the possibilities for identifying with people—whether they are voluntary immigrants, refugees or asylum seekers—who have come to a land that is strange to them, where they have considerable problems with the culture, language and way of living. Since the figures on the stage with whom the audience expect to be able to identify speak a barely understandable language an increasing understanding for the particular situation of the immigrants develops. The "newcomer" Nick, who has to learn English in this play, has no idea how he is to cope in the face of the new culture and the—for him—incomprehensible language. The pupils at his school tease him because he is different. The audience hears the thoughts of the "New Canadian" and is at the same time confronted with the speech of Canadians that it understands just as little as Nick.

What is important for Foon is the situation with which immigrants—wherever they move to—see themselves confronted with. Nick comes from a very specific, if imaginary, country that is known simply as "Homeland." Superficially the mother and her son are supposed to appear foreign to the Canadians. Yet their clothing may not be permitted to show any sort of identification with any particular country. Foon's own recommendation is that Nick should be dressed in differing nuances of green and the Canadians should wear other colours. Later, as Nick begins to feel more at home in Canada, these other colours should become a constituent part of his clothing.

New Canadian Kid's universal message makes it a highly recommendable piece for the stage, especially in countries which have populations of immigrants. It has already been put on in England, Denmark, Sweden, Hong Kong, Singapore, Australia, New Zealand and in the USA. The fact that Dennis Foon did not write *New Canadian Kid* specifically for a Canadian audience was made all the more clear when the play was later renamed simply *New Kid*.

More than a million schoolchildren have taken up this play with great enthusiasm. Nick is their mouthpiece. Through him they are able to articulate their opinions and also their attitudes towards grownups, particularly their parents. Nick is also the foreign pupil in their schoolyard who, in an unfamiliar cultural and social environment, searches for a new identity. As Susan Patrick explains, *New Canadian Kid* "advocates tolerance, humanity, hope and optimism, and is recommended for introducing some important issues to elementary-school-age children in an entertaining fashion." (*Canadian Book Review* 1991, 244)

Dennis Foon lives in Vancouver. He is Canada's most prominent author of stage plays for young theatregoers. He received the British Theatre Award for his play *Invisible Kids* and for his drama *Skin* he was awarded the Chalmers Award. He is also widely known for his work as a director and founded the Green Thumb Theatre in Vancouver. It may also be of interest to enthusiasts of German theatre that he has adapted two plays by the Berliner Grips Theater: *Trummi Kaput* and *Bedtimes and Bullies*.

Themes
- The isolation of immigrants in society
- Language problems and culture shock
- Multiculturalism
- Racism and xenophobia
- Relationships between adults and children

Some other plays

Available from Playwrights Canada Press:
- *Hindsight*
- *Little Criminals* (screenplay)
- *Mirror Game*
- *Short Tree and the Bird that Could not Sing*
- *Skin & Liars* (two plays)
- *Seesaw*

Available from Playwrights Guild of Canada:
- *Bedtimes and Bullies*
- *The Hunchback of Notre Dame*
- *Mirror Games* (one-act version)
- *Sunspots*
- *Trummi Kaput*
- *Zaydok*

Available from Arsenal Pulp Press:
- *New Canadian Kid* (in *New Canadian Kid and Invisible Kids*)

Available from Talonbooks:
- *Heracles*
- *Raft Baby*
- *Windigo*

Unidentified Human Remains and the True Nature of Love

Brad Fraser

Premiere: 1989, *PlayRites '89 New Play Festival*, production by *Alberta Theatre Projects*, Calgary, Alberta

Director: Bob White

Cast: 7 (3 women, 4 men)

Stage Setting: Various locations in Edmonton, Alberta including an apartment, a bar and a restaurant

Publisher/Place/Year: Blizzard Publishing, Winnipeg, Manitoba 1990; In *Love and Human Remains/Unidentified Human Remains and the True Nature of Love*, NeWest Press, Edmonton, Alberta 1996

Length: 95 pages

Performance rights: Shain Jaffe, Great North Artists, 350 Dupont Street, Toronto, Ontario M5R 1V9, 416-925-2051, fax 416-925-3904

Characters
DAVID
CANDY
BERNIE
KANE
ROBERT
JERRI
BENITA

Summary

The play thematizes the unconnectedness of people in front of a backdrop of modern life in the Canadian city of Edmonton. Candy is looking for love. She is, however, unable to build up a relationship with either David, who is married, or Jerri, who is a lesbian. David does not believe in love. Benita offers perverts the opportunity of practising their predilections and analyses her friends using her telepathic abilities. Kane is fascinated by David, who is gay, and cannot get him out of his mind although he himself is not gay. Finally, there is Bernie who is cheating on his wife.

In Brad Fraser's one-act play there is no division into scenes. All the events are somehow woven into each other, dialogues take place simultaneously, and there is only to a certain extent a continuous plot. The characters wend their way in a disoriented fashion through the "wounded city" (to quote Bernie), each of them is on his or her own search for some sort of foothold in society. Violence is ever present: in the characters' speech, in Benita's fondness for gruesome murder stories and in the person of a serial killer who is killing young women in Edmonton. At the end it turns out to be Bernie. David considers shooting him with a gun, but then finds himself unable to murder his best friend and leaves him alone with the weapon. When Bernie realises that even David, who has always stood by him, is going to leave him and is ready to turn him in to the police he shoots himself.

Bernie's death and his terrible secret shock David to the very core. He withdraws into himself, hardly eating or speaking, and stares for hours into space. But he is not alone: Candy and Kane are there, other friends call him up, and very slowly David begins to open up again and to feel trust again. The last sentence of the play—spoken by Benita—is: "I love you." It expresses that despite the sombre and sometimes even threatening atmosphere there is a glimmer of hope even when there is no happy end.

Background and Commentary

The divided and elaborate sounding title *Unidentified Human Remains and the True Nature of Love* can be understood as a question rather than a statement: which aspects of human nature are still left for us to discover? Where, if at all, can one find true love in today's society?

Brad Fraser's play is on the one hand a furious examination of broken-down human relationships (one thinks of John Osborne's *Look Back in Anger*) and on the other hand a bluntly open, but also sympathetic portrait of the life of young homosexuals and heterosexuals in the eighties.

Brad Fraser grew up in a hard-bitten working class area of Edmonton (his father worked for a construction company). He had one of the worst childhoods that one can imagine. He and the other members of his family were terrorised and humiliated by his father and he was sexually abused by one of his cousins. He is bisexual, and as such "outed" himself several years ago.

The origin of *Unidentified Human Remains and the True Nature of Love* was the brutal slaying in Edmonton in 1986 of a young woman, Brenda McLenaghan, who was discovered bound with a long cord to a tree. This terrible deed horrifies the residents of Edmonton even to this day and has led to increased alertness among the residents.

Hardly any play in the past few years has caused such a furor and discussion or aroused such a divided reaction amongst the critics in the way that this piece from Fraser has. Some call it an "urban drama" about sex, love, death and violence in the nineties. Others are disgusted and horrified by some of the scenes about misdirected sexuality. Yet others consider it to be the story of (mainly young) people in our time who seek contact with others but never find it.

Unidentified Human Remains and the True Nature of Love is a provocative play that asks a lot of its audience, because it portrays a violent world, a world bereft of sense, in which seven young people are terrorised by a serial killer. They are all on a search for something that will give their lives sense and purpose and no one can help them but themselves. They are not particularly bothered by terror and murder but in their relationships they are disoriented and at a psychological low. They consider romantic love to be a relic of the bourgeois society. One-night stands, drugs, beer, punk rock and mobile telephones control their lives. They are no longer capable of finding love.

Brad Fraser has succeeded with *Unidentified Human Remains and the True Nature of Love* in luring young people in droves to the theatre – young people who otherwise had scarcely seen a play on the stage. One may perhaps criticise him that through the portrayal of his cynical and hedonistic protagonists he is cleverly exploiting a need in theatregoers for sensationalism, that he is mockingly teasing out desires of varying types and that with his use of a particular vernacular he is making an offer of identification (particularly to the young). However, what is certain is that Fraser speaks the language of his generation and by avoiding splitting his play into scenes, instead allowing simultaneous dialogue to create a filmic feel to the action, he has really hit on the particular tastes of his audience – a fact not lost on Louis Hobson who reviewed the first production of *Unidentified Human Remains and the True Nature of Love* for the *Calgary Sun* (12th January 1989), and remarked:

> Fraser juggles language with amazing skill. The jokes effortlessly spin off each other, then break away for some deadly insights. He is unquestionably as astute an observer as he is a skilled technician of word play.

The cinematic construction of *Unidentified Human Remains and the True Nature of Love* gave rise to the idea of turning the play into a film, for which Fraser then wrote the screenplay. The director of the film was **Denys** Arcand, who was already well known for his films *Jesus of Montréal* and *The Decline of the American Empire*. The stage play has, in the meantime, also been produced in Britain. *Unidentified Human Remains and the True Nature of Love* is a mirror onto contemporary patterns of behaviour; partly a romance, partly a horror-story, it also subliminally reveals that often the way people treat each other borders on psycho-terror. The messages on the answering machine are more communicative than the people are when they meet each other. With *Unidentified Human Remains and the True Nature of Love* Fraser was able to make a breakthrough which, in the words of Julia Nunes in *The Globe and Mail* "allowed him to defeat both his personal demons and the conservatism of the commercial theatre."

Themes
- The senselessness of the modern world
- The attempts of the individual to find orientation in a major city
- Alienation in the urban jungle
- Love versus violence
- Perversion and excessive sexuality

Some other plays
Available from NeWest Press:
- *Martin Yesterday*
- *Poor Super Man*
- *Snake in the Fridge*
- *The Ugly Man*
- *Wolfboy* (in *The Wolf Plays*)

Jitters

David French

Premiere: 16th February 1979, *Tarragon Theatre*, Toronto, Ontario
Director: Bill Glassco
Cast: 9 (3 women, 6 men)
Stage Setting: Various locations including a middle-class living room and a dressing room
Publisher/Place/Year: Talonbooks, Vancouver, British Columbia 1980
Length: 140 pages
Performance rights: Charles Northcote, The Core Group Talent Agency Inc., 507-3 Church St., Toronto, Ontario, 416-955-0819, fax 416-955-0861

Characters
PATRICK FLANAGAN: 50 years old
JESSICA LOGAN: 50 years old
PHIL MASTORAKIS: 44 years old
GEORGE ELLSWORTH: 30 years old
ROBERT ROSS: 26 years old
TOM KENT: 22 years old
NICK: 28 years old
SUSI: 23 years old
PEGGY: 20 years old

Summary

Jitters is a "play within a play." A theatre group is about to premiere the comedy *The Care and Treatment of Roses*. All the players are very nervous and there are many arguments, which finally become the pressure valve for all their nervousness. Another cause for the squabbling and exacerbated worry is a certain Mr. Feldman from New York, a famous producer who has announced that he will be there on the opening night. All the players are hoping to be "discovered" by him. On the day of the premiere the degree of stage fright has reached its zenith, especially seeing as on this of all evenings a number of extraordinary incidents occur. Phil turns up late at the theatre, sporting a black eye that he has acquired in a brawl. Tom also arrives late and, to top it all off, is inebriated. Thus curtain-up is delayed while they attempt to sober him up a little. In the end, however, the performance is a success for most of those involved. The press heaps beneficent praise upon the play, direction and the performers – with the exception of Jessica, who they tear to pieces. In the hope of being noticed by Feldman all the actors have made an extra effort to be good, which, in the case of Jessica, the press consider to be negative and artificial. Jessica considers for a short while whether she has a future at all in theatre. All the others are, on the other hand, very pleased. Then George, the director, shares with them that Feldman had actually cancelled his visit because of flight delays. This announcement provokes great disappointment among the others who had set their sights on being discovered by the great producer.

Background and Commentary

Jitters is a "comedy-of-the-stage." When the curtain is raised there is already a performance in progress, a play within a play, which serves as a good peg on which to hang the thoroughly amusing rehearsal scenes and the private goings-on of the actors behind the scenes. Ambiguous situations arise when the actors then make their way to the front of the stage to slip into their intended "roles."

This comedy joins a group of well-known plays, such as the English playwright Michael Frayn's *Noises Off*, which incidentally was written three years after *Jitters*. An example from America is *A Life in the Theater*, which was written by the successful playwright David Mamet in the middle of the seventies. A final example that one might mention is Peter Shaffer's *Black Comedy*.

In all of these plays it is the events on the stage *and* behind the scenes which constitute the subject of the performance. In addition to that, *Jitters* is a play with a particularly Canadian pattern of behaviour and a particularly Canadian take on theatre. This comedy marked an important phase in the development of modern Canadian theatre. It shows clearly the efforts that Canadian theatre people made in the seventies to emancipate themselves from Broadway and the West End. It shows also, however, how Canadian theatre was able to laugh at itself in the meantime. David French himself made the following comment about the play:

> The play is about jitters, fears, failure and success[…] however, the figures are rooted in Canadian reality. […]I criticise specifically Canadian attitudes [*at the beginning of the eighties* (Albert-Reiner Glaap)], like, for instance, the demand that you had to be recognised first and foremost in New York, because without that recognition you didn't count, because it was thought that without the American stamp of approval you wouldn't go far.

There are many plays about the theatre or the theatre as the mirror of life. What is special about *Jitters* is that David French has brought new life to the well-known genre of comedy-of-the-stage by breathing in a breath of Canadian-ness. For that reason if not any other is *Jitters* a play that can be recommended for productions abroad because by means of comedy it gives an insight into how Canadians think and behave.

Themes
- Metadrama with a look behind the scenes of the theatre world
- American theatre as a yardstick for Canada (in the seventies)
- The search for success and recognition
- Theatre as a medium and subject for presentation (see also Peter Shaffer, *Black Comedy*; Michael Frayn, *Noises Off*)

Some other plays
Available from Talonbooks:
- *Leaving Home*
- *1949*
- *Salt-Water Moon*
- *The Seagull*
- *Silver Dagger*
- *Soldier's Heart*
- *That Summer*

Les Guerriers/ Warriors

Michel Garneau

Premiere (Fr.): 6th April 1989, *L'Atelier du Centre National des Arts*, Ottawa, Ontario; co-production by the *Théâtre d'Aujourd'hui* and the *Théâtre Français du Centre National des Arts*
Director: Guy Beausoleil
Premiere (Eng.): 25th January 1990, *Martha Cohen Theatre*, Calgary, Alberta; co-production by the *Alberta Theatre Projects*, Calgary, Alberta *(PlayRites '90 Festival)* and the *Belfry Theatre*, Victoria, British Columbia
Director: Glynis Leyshon
Cast: 2 men
Stage Setting: A high-tech office in an advertising agency
Publisher/Place/Year: (Fr.) VLB Éditeur, Montréal, Québec 1989; (Eng.) Talonbooks, Vancouver, British Columbia 1990
Running time: 1 hour 40
Performance rights: Des Landes, Dickinson et associés, 4171 Hampton Avenue, Montréal, Québec H4A 2L1

Characters
GILLES
PAUL

Summary

At the end of the eighties advertising copywriter Gilles and his boss Paul are working under great pressure in a modern advertising studio on a lucrative advertising campaign for the Canadian army.

This short-notice contract has to be finished within nine days and Paul has already collected copious amounts of source material and literature on the subject of war. Gilles is not entirely in favour of taking the contract but has let himself be tempted by the prospect of a two-year paid sabbatical as a reward. The necessity of portraying the Army as something positive forces the two into an intensive examination of the themes "War" and "The Military."

For the duration of their work the two seal themselves off in their studio thereby cutting themselves off from the possibility of outside distractions by providing themselves with ample rations and pulling out the telephone cable. Alcohol and cocaine serve as stimulants.

Gilles, by means of the books he has in his possession, intensively researches the subject of war. But again and again he is troubled by intense chest pains – a clear indication of his coming heart attack. He is very critical of the superficial nature of the advertising scene, yet he is unable to escape. When, on the third day, the flash of inspiration for the campaign has still not appeared Gilles and Paul get into a verbal battle with each other so that they both become "warriors" – with words as weapons. Gilles proves to be quicker and more inventive than Paul, who denies having the intention of coming up with a slogan himself anyway. Naturally both are only capable of making gruesome and awful associations with the word "war." Gilles is repeatedly troubled by pain, but denies that he is seriously ill.

The next day both men examine the nature of their relationship and discuss who is trying to manipulate whom. They both agree that they need each other. Later, on day six, both men's thoughts begin to converge as they come up with the idea of making naive and unspoiled children the target group for their campaign. A further nuance of the campaign is that it is to have a religious feel to it.

The already inflamed mood of the two men is further pepped up with Scotch and cocaine. But they still lack a catchy slogan. Influenced by this working atmosphere Paul admits that he feels that he is living a vacuous, emotionless life and that his surroundings are utterly unimportant to him. The two copywriters are turning mental circles around each other and are no closer to finding a solution although the deadline is inexorably approaching.

Finally—on the eighth day—Gilles develops the sobering thought that you can find the army "in the yellow pages" just like any other business, but Paul rejects his idea.

On the ninth and last day the two are again propping up their ever more fragile moods by means of drugs. Paul quite suddenly tells his colleague that his father died in the war when Paul was still a baby. He rather unheroically blew himself to pieces with a grenade. Gilles' father's only contribution to the war had been that, towards the end, he had riveted tanks together. This recollection of the past, however, brings the two no comfort.

When Gilles, who is by this time exhausted, announces that he is going to stop and will no longer finish the project Paul threatens him with a revolver. This, however, does not impress Gilles and Paul lowers the weapon. As they talk on Gilles confirms Paul's suspicion that the two men's wives are sleeping with each other. Paul is prepared to let Gilles go as he decides to use Gilles' idea about the yellow pages. Just at this moment Gilles suffers a massive heart attack and collapses dragging Paul down with him. Paul assures his dying friend that they will after all use the slogan "We're in the Yellow Pages." For Gilles, however, this small victory comes too late – he dies in Paul's arms.

Background Commentary

Les Guerriers (or *Warriors* in Linda Gaboriau's English translation of the play) leads the audience into the world of advertising, a world where everything—even war—is treated as a product. This is a two-man play: Gilles is the copywriter and Paul is his manager. Both are specialists in an advertising agency. Paul has managed to land a very important contract from the Canadian Army on the condition that he can lay a concept on the table at the end of a week. With the prospect of two years fully-paid leave Gilles, who at first is very much against taking on the job, declares himself willing to attempt the task. Their brief is to come up with a slogan to replace the current one (*Si la vie vous intéresse*) and which should impart the idea that the business of war is good for young people. Gilles is the creative element of the partnership, the ideas man. Paul is the businessman, the opportunist, devoid of feelings, the "slave-driver" who attempts to get Gilles going with Chivas Regal and cocaine. Both are driven by the need for success. They are given ten days to complete the contract. In each of the play's nine scenes (Day One to Day Nine) only the decisive moments of the working day are presented. The action itself takes place in a large apartment with mirrors on the walls, microwaves, televisions, computers and exercise machines all around. At the beginning Gilles is manipulated by Paul but his own behaviour becomes increasingly Machiavellian throughout the play. Co-operation turns into confrontation and then finally into physical aggression. Finally Gilles has the decisive idea which he then develops into the slogan "*Nous sommes dans les Pages Jaunes*" ("We're in the Yellow Pages"). The Army belongs in the Yellow Pages because it is just as much a business as any other firm, or business.

The play can be understood on several different levels. One level is how we can understand or interpret the ambiguous relationship between Gilles and Paul. Another is the way in which *Les Guerriers* thematizes the *modus operandi* of Québécois advertising agencies in the 1980s which almost exclusively used French translations of English/American advertising slogans. They were often of lesser quality, often sounded a little ridiculous and were also considered by some of the French-speaking Québécois as an insult. Or, as Jean Beaunover in *La Presse*, put it: "*Comment vendre la guerre par la publicité?* That is the question, *aurait dit Shakespeare à une autre époque.*" (*La Presse*, Montréal, 30th April 1989) On a third level Alberta Theatre Projects declared that they wanted to perform this play (in 1990) to highlight Canada's indifference to theatre in Québec.

It may well be that it is the intention of *Les Guerriers* to clarify certain facets of Canada's cultural "crisis" in the eighties by using advertising as a symptomatic example of the age. What is certain is that Garneau's play is, as Pat Donnelly wrote in the *Gazette* in May 1989, "the call of the pacifist in the wilderness who is warning us about the terrible consequences of materialism." At times the play seems also to be addressing the problem of writer's block, that occasional barrier to a writer's creative process when he is—for a certain amount of time at least—unable to write anything of worth. This problem is raised frequently during the play's duration.

Michel Garneau (born 1939) is a highly respected dramatist, poet and translator. By the time he was just fifteen he was already working in the media as a radio commentator and announcer. Since then he has written many series for radio and television. Most of his plays (which number at around forty so far) have been performed in Québec. In January 1989 he was awarded the Governor General's Award for *Mademoiselle Rouge*, a play for young audiences.

Themes
- Advertising in the consumer society
- Creativity versus commerciality
- Hierarchy in working life
- Businessman versus artist
- Desire to make profit and personal morality

Some other plays
- *Mademoiselle Rouge* (VLB Éditeur)
  Miss Red and the Wolves – translated by Linda Gaboriau (CEAD and Factory Theatre, Toronto)
- *Héleotropes* (VLB Éditeur)
  Morning Glories – translated by Linda Gaboriau (CEAD and Factory Theatre, Toronto)

Sky

Connie Gault

Premiere: February 1989, *25th Street Theatre Centre*, Saskatoon, Saskatchewan

Director: Tom Bentley-Fisher

Cast: 4 (3 women, 1 man)

Stage Setting: Various locations in the vicinity of a small prairie town including a room, a house, a garden (at the edge of the garden there is a metal archway), a kitchen window with old curtains and a view into the garden and its archway, a simple kitchen, a bedroom; late summer and winter 1920-22

Publisher/Place/Year: Blizzard Publishing, Winnipeg, Manitoba 1989; Scirocco, Winnipeg, Manitoba 2002

Length: 79 pages

Performance rights: Connie Gault through Playwrights Canada Press

Characters

BLANCHE: 16 years old; married to Jasper; pregnant; uses a surface anger to screen herself from others

JASPER: late twenties; an honest man with a sense of humour

NELL: mid-thirties; a lively, motherly woman

OLD BLANCHE: a strong and resolute old woman; chain smoker

Summary

Blanche, a sixteen-year-old who is expecting her father's child, marries Jasper. Up to this point the two have never even seen each other. Jasper is very considerate to Blanche but a bit "prickly." She swears and curses and attempts to cut herself off from the outside world. She tells the somewhat naive Jasper that the child she is expecting is God's and that the Lord's child will be born at Christmas. Although hesitant at first, Jasper slowly begins to believe that his wife has been chosen by God.

On Christmas day—and therefore on the day of confinement—Blanche and Jasper's neighbour, Nell, who has from day one tried to look after Blanche but who has always been turned away, makes a tragic discovery. While examining Blanche she discovers that the baby in Blanche's womb is dead. Blanche reacts to the news hysterically but then finally tells Nell the truth about the child. It was her father's, he had abused her. Nell is, however, clearly not totally surprised.

After this "revelation" Nell puts Blanche back to bed without telling Jasper about the baby's death. He attempts to stay awake all night in case he is needed to help with the child's delivery. Finally, however, he does fall asleep.

The next day, seeing as Blanche has still not given birth to the child, Jasper, who still believes that Christ is about to return, is at his wit's end and is very critical of both himself and his wife. Blanche comforts him and takes him in her arms—something she has never done before—and insists that the blame lies solely with her.

This poignant story is told throughout by "Old Blanche," many years later as she looks back at her life.

Background and Commentary

Sky was Connie Gault's first stage play in 1989. Previously the author had won recognition through her many radio plays and her collection of short stories, *Some of Eve's Daughters*. She comes originally from Central Butte in the province of Saskatchewan but lives now in Regina. As a child she heard the story of a sixteen-year-old who was forced to marry shortly after the First World War in order to cover up a pregnancy which had arisen through incest. "I wrote *Sky* because I couldn't get this story out of my head," Gault herself said.

The content of this play is not the only thing that is of interest to audiences at the end of the twentieth century. The time and place of the action (*Sky* takes place in the Canadian prairie) are far away from the actuality of our everyday lives. However, the style and the message of this play have made it into a very popular piece. It captivates through the simplicity of its language and construction; it concentrates exclusively on the relationship between Blanche and her twenty-year-old husband Jasper. A particular challenge for any director of this play is that as well as the sixteen-year-old Blanche he must find someone to plausibly play the older version, Old Blanche, who is one and the same person.

   Sky can be understood on different levels. On the one hand it presents us with a picture of small-town life on the prairie. It deals with the innocence of two victims of a society which is paralysed by conventions and religious constraints, but also with the courage and the strength of those people who have to live in the bleak and monotonous landscape of the prairie. It thematizes the causes and consequences of sexual abuse. On another level *Sky* expounds the problems of personal relationships within marriage and also among friends. Finally it also looks at the relationship between the existences of a person in her youth and in later life. *Sky* is thus much more than the story of two misfits who have been married off to each other solely to keep two problem cases from coming to light.

Themes
• Child abuse and incest
• Reappraisal of one's own past
• Life in the barrenness of the prairie
• Constraints of convention and courage of independence

Some other plays
Available from Coteau Books:
• *The Snow Dream*

Available from Scirocco:
• *Otherwise Bob* (also in *7 Cannons*, Playwrights Canada Press, Toronto)
• *Soft Eclipse*

*Billy Bishop
Goes to War*

John Gray/
Eric Peterson

Premiere: 3ʳᵈ November 1978, *Vancouver East Cultural Centre*, Vancouver, British Columbia; co-production by the *Vancouver East Cultural Centre* and the *Tamahnous Theatre*

Director: John Gray

Cast: 18 (2 women, 16 men) plus the narrator/pianist. One actor plays the roles of all 18 characters and is accompanied by the narrator/pianist

Stage Setting: Various locations including officers' mess, the war ministry etc.

Publisher/Place/Year: Talonbooks, Vancouver, British Columbia 1980

Length: 102 pages

Performance rights: Beverlee Miller Gray, johngray@telus.net

Characters

BILLY BISHOP, UPPERCLASSMAN, ADJUTANT PERRAULT, OFFICER, SIR HUGH CECIL, LADY ST. HELIER, CEDRIC, DOCTOR, INSTRUCTOR, GENERAL JOHN HIGGINS, TOMMY, LOVELY HELENE, ALBERT BALL, WALTER BOURNE, GERMAN, GENERAL HUGH M. TRENCHARD, SERVANT, KING GEORGE V

Summary

The twenty-year-old Canadian Billy Bishop attracts trouble like a magnet. When he gets into trouble again at the Royal Military College during the First World War he decides to volunteer for military service in Europe to avoid his punishment. Once in Europe he quickly recognises the seriousness of the situation and decides to spend the rest of the war in hospital, a plan which is, at first, successful. Then an old lady friend of his father arranges for his release from hospital intending to help him. She manages to get him a position in the Royal Flying Corps as a pilot and builds him up to be a model soldier.

After his first kill Billy begins to enjoy his new life; he has, so to speak, "tasted blood" and breaks all the records as a fighter pilot. Finally he single-handedly attacks a German base, destroys it and escapes unharmed. At the pinnacle of his career it is decided—initially against his will—to send him home. A live hero is more useful for maintaining morale than a dead one. Billy flies just a couple more missions and during his last dogfight with a German flier he has a strange experience: he sees the enemy plane break up before his eyes and its crew fall to their deaths although he is sure he hadn't even hit their plane. Suddenly he begins to have doubts about what he is doing. Finally he is pleased that he can return to Canada.

Yet twenty years later, when the authorities are looking for volunteers to fight in the Second World War, he encourages his son to apply for service and makes a rousing speech.

Background and Commentary

Billy Bishop, the hero of the play, was born in Owen Sound, Ontario in 1894, the son of a lawyer. At the age of seventeen he became a cadet at the Royal Military College in Kingston. In 1915 he began training for infantry service at the front in France. However, he had very soon had enough of the mud in the trenches and decided to try for the Flying Corps and trained as a pilot. In the last two years of the war he managed 72 kills of enemy aircraft and became the most successful allied pilot of the war, the allied equivalent of Baron von Richthofen, so to speak. After the war Bishop founded a company selling civil aircraft, which was closed down a short time later. In the thirties he became involved in the oil business and at the beginning of the Second World War he ran one of the Commonwealth training centres in Canada. Towards the end of the war he resumed his career as an oilman. He died in 1956 in Palm Beach, Florida.

The starting point for Gray and Peterson's play was a book written by the twenty-one-year-old Bishop himself, *Winged Warfare* (1918), in which the flier describes his first six kills in the First World War. Eric Peterson discovered the book in 1976 and recommended it to John Gray. Many discussions on the theme followed and the two spent the next two years researching the subject, mainly in military archives. In the summer of

1978 Gray began work on the play itself. A rough version was ready as early as the following March and a theatre in Ottawa provided money for a workshop.

Winged Warfare answered many questions at that time, such as: how did a Canadian become the most successful flying ace of the war when Canada had never really had anything to do with war or warfare? How did Bishop rationalise his career as a pilot with the almost proverbial Canadian inferiority complex? But in *Billy Bishop Goes to War* the question is not whether or why this or that war was good or bad. It is, in the words of Jo Ledingham, "a visual reminder of the confusion surrounding the nature of heroism; we deplore war, yet decorate its heroes and continue to be entertained—sometimes with song and dance—by tales of glory." (*Georgia Straight*, Feb. 2-9, 1990). John Gray is trying to make it clear in this play that "war is like life, only quicker. If you survive you find out how your friends die." The play, as it says in the foreword of the printed edition is "dedicated to all those who didn't come back from the war, and to all those who did and wondered why."

John Gray is a representative of Canadian musical drama that cannot really be classified alongside the big American musicals like *Oklahoma* or *Annie Get Your Gun*. Gray was born in Nova Scotia in 1946 and later became—along with his two brothers—a professional musician. His first play, which he directed himself, was called *18 Wheels*. In it long-haul truckers and waitresses tell each other their stories in country and western music.

Gray says of himself that he has a highly developed sense of hearing, but no "eye" to filter out of a certain context what it is that the audience likes. For that reason he didn't want to write any plays in which music didn't play a fundamental role. Eric Peterson's enthusiasm for historical details and his interest in local and temporal specifics were in this case an important complement. His dramatic artistic contribution was of fundamental importance to the play's success. Peterson comes from the prairie province of Saskatchewan.

Themes
• Canada's role in the First World War
• Heroism and patriotism
• Glorification of war

Some other plays
Available from Talonbooks:
• *Don Messer's Jubilee*
• *18 Wheels*
• *Rock and Roll*

The Rez Sisters

Tomson Highway

Premiere: 26th November 1986, *Native Canadian Centre of Toronto*; co-production by the *Act IV Theatre Company* and *Native Earth Performing Arts Inc.*

Director: Larry Lewis

Cast: 10 (7 women, 3 men) All the male roles are played by the same actor

Stage Setting: Various locations in the *Wasaychigan Hill* Indian reserve, Manitoulin Island, Ontario; late summer 1986

Publisher/Place/Year: Fifth House Publishers, Saskatoon, Saskatchewan 1988

Length: 118 pages

Performance rights: Suzanne DePoe, Toronto, Ontario, 416-944-0475, fax 416-944-0136 suzanne@wcaltd.com

Characters

PELAJIA PATCHNOSE: 53 years old

PHILOMENA MOOSETAIL: 49 years old; Pelajia's sister

MARIE-ADELE STARBLANKET: 39 years old; half sister to Pelajia and Philomena

ANNIE COOK: 36 years old; Marie-Adele's sister and half-sister to the other two

EMILY DICTIONARY: 32 years old; Annie's sister and half-sister to Pelajia and Philomena

VERONIQUE ST. PIERRE: 45 years old; sister-in-law to the others

ZHABOONIGAN PETERSON: 24 years old; Veronique's mentally handicapped daughter
NANABUSH: mythological Indian figure; plays the seagull (in white), the nighthawk (in black) and the Bingo Master

Summary

Pelajia, Philomena, Marie-Adele, Annie, Emily, Veronique and her daughter decide to travel to the biggest "Bingo in the World" in Toronto. They are all convinced that a big win will solve all their problems. Philomena dreams of a modern bathroom with a WC, Pelajia wants to have the dusty streets paved in the reservation where they all live, Marie-Adele wants to buy an island for herself and her family, Annie wants all of Patsy Cline's records and Veronique a new stove. The women themselves are as individual as their wishes are different. Quite unlike a band of blood-sisters the women argue constantly, insult one another, pinch each other's men and try to survive the living conditions on the reservation through their sheer energy levels.

During the trip to Toronto, the audience discovers that Philomena has had an abortion and that Emily has witnessed her girlfriend being killed by a truck. While the women make a rest stop Marie-Adele meets Nanabush, the Nighthawk, who appears as an omen of her imminent death.

The bingo itself proves to be only a partial success. Only Philomena wins and she is able to buy her dream bathroom, but the trip has influenced the lives of all the women in different ways. Marie-Adele dies, Veronique takes care of Marie-Adele's husband and fourteen children and thus indirectly she does get her hands on a new cooker. Emily is overjoyed when she finds out she is pregnant and Annie becomes a singer in her lover's band Fritz the Katz. Yet life on the reservation is still just as poor and forgotten by society as ever, but it is clear that the women now fight harder than ever not to let it bring them down.

Background and Commentary

Tomson Highway was born in a tent "in the middle of a snowbank on his father's trap line," on a remote island in north Manitoba. He was the second youngest of twelve children and until the age of six only spoke Cree, his tribal language. Then he was sent—at the behest of the government—to the Roman Catholic boarding school for Natives in The Pas. He was only allowed to return home in the summer months. The bad experiences he had in school caused him to reject the Catholic religion and turn to the spirituality of his forefathers. This was a decisive point in the development of his understanding of "inspiration." The events in his plays are determined by the actions of one central character who derives from Native mythology, the Trickster, who is neither exclusively a male or a female figure rather one or the other or both. In Highway's understanding, the Trickster is a figure—somewhat like Jesus—who is half man, half god – a heroic figure. He still lives today. You can feel his presence not only on the reservations but also in the big shopping malls. He interferes in the lives and deeds of man. He is, in Highway's words: "Like a magic dust which is scattered over our daily lives and transforms them into something wonderful." The Trickster and other mythological figures are archetypes which everyone can appreciate – regardless of their origin, race or religion.

These days the author lives in Toronto. Editions of his works are available from the Playwrights Guild of Canada. *The Rez Sisters* (Rez being an abbreviation for reservation), his best-known work so far (1986) became a ground-breaking work in the development of indigenous theatre in Canada, because Highway brought the figure of Nanabush onto the stage and in so doing showed that the thinking of the Canadian First Nations Peoples could be carried over into our lives and have meaning for us too. "I decided to live in the city," says Highway "and in order that the legends retain their meaning for my current life I have to attempt to relate them to the reality of city life." One facet of this view expresses itself in the fact that he and other Native writers write in English, albeit in an English that they have remodelled to suit their own purposes.

Up until the sixties, plays about First Nations People were still being written as a rule by non-Native authors. These days the indigenous authors articulate their own standpoints, views and problems. A weighty argument that Highway, Taylor and Moses (all featured in this book) use that only Natives should and can write about Natives is this: drama is, in their understanding, a continuation of the oral tradition, which touches on the wisdom of the elders and is therefore, as far as they are concerned, the centre of the Native cultural identity. Their mythology found its expression in its oral format long before Columbus set foot on the American continent in 1492. Contemporary Canadian drama no longer restricts itself to works in English and French. The works of indigenous dramatists now constitute a considerable proportion of the works produced which are received well even in Europe; not least because they transfer the oral myths and traditions of the First Nations Peoples into our modern world. The insights that these often experimental Native works grant us can directly give us understanding of a culture that is at first a little alien to us and can indirectly contribute to intercultural understanding.

Nancy Wigston begins her article "Nanabush in the City" in *Books in Canada* (March 1989) with the following sentence: "Tomson Highway writes in English, dreams in Cree and his works combine his knowledge of Native realities in his country with classical structures and artistic language."

Themes
- Elements of Native mythology
- Meaning and function of the Trickster figure
- Ghettoization of minorities
- The life of women on the reservation
- Realisation of dreams and hopes
- Bingo as a game and an elixir of life

Also by this author
Available from Fifth House:
- *Dry Lips Oughta Move to Kapuskasing*

Aurélie, My Sister/Aurélie, ma sœur

Marie Laberge

Premiere (French): 1ˢᵗ November 1988, *Grand Théâtre*, Québec City, Québec; production by the *Théâtre du Trident*
Director: Marie Laberge
Premiere (Eng.): Translation commissioned for the *Interact 89*, the translation was a co-production of CEAD and *Factory Theatre*, Toronto, Ontario 1989
Cast: 2 women
Stage Setting: conservatory of a house in Montréal, Québec; 1983/84
Publisher/Place/Year: (Fr.) VLB Éditeur, Outremont, Québec 1988; (Eng.) Centre des Auteurs Dramatiques, Montréal, Québec 1989 (Rehearsal Draft)
Running Time: 2 hours 20

Characters

AURÉLIE: 45 years old at the beginning of the play; a woman of great humanity, compassion and perceptiveness; unsentimental; treats Cat/Chatte as a friend; mother-daughter overtones between the two women should be avoided, rather the tenderness and understanding between the two women should be emphasised.

CHATTE (in French version)/CAT (in English version): 23 years old at the beginning of the play; her real name is Charlotte; she is lively and passionate. No half measures for her, she lives life to the limit; much more than a pretty girl, she has great inner beauty and a commitment to life.

Summary

The play presents in five acts, each representing different meetings over a time period of several years, the fate, the past and the current relationship between Aurélie, in her mid-forties, and the younger Charlotte, known as Chatte (Cat in the English version).

At the beginning of the play one assumes that the two women are an aunt and her niece. Aurélie, a teacher, has been divorced for eighteen years and lives in a house in Montréal. The action of the play takes place in the conservatory of this house. The beautiful Cat has fallen in love with a married man with children, Pierre-Louis, whom Aurélie with all her experience of life mistrusts.

Aurélie writes regularly to her sister Charlotte who works as a sculptress in Italy providing detailed reports about Cat's development. Charlotte, however, never writes back. Charlotte left many years previously and Aurélie has taken over the mother role from her.

During further meetings of the two women, who are extremely fond of each other, it becomes clear that Cat's relationship to Pierre-Louis and his separation from his family is proving to be rather difficult. After many ups and downs, Cat is able to make a clean break from him. Aurélie sympathises with Cat's suffering and is reminded of her own experiences with men, love and sexuality.

Aurélie has hoped for years that her sister would invite her to Italy – in vain. She has felt an emptiness in her since Charlotte's move to Italy, as her life had been, up to this point, centred on her sister.

The fourth meeting directly follows the funeral of Aurélie's father, which Charlotte does not attend. Slowly something comes to light, which the audience should have already begun to suspect, namely that Aurélie's father and Cat's father are in fact one and the same person. Many years ago he had made his own daughter, Charlotte, pregnant and this had irrevocably changed the nature of his relationship with Aurélie although he had never actually laid a finger on her. From then on Aurélie had attempted to forget and disparage her rather simple and uneducated—but up to that point good—father. His abuse of Charlotte brings her into a conflict with herself: all the good qualities which she had inherited from him she suppresses. It is only when she lays him to rest that she is finally able to also bury the little girl in her that had always loved her daddy. She still suffers from feelings of guilt towards her younger sister whom she feels she should have protected from her father. When Charlotte left she had made Aurélie promise solemnly that their father would never be allowed to touch Cat. Aurélie only then lets Cat in on the secret because it is the only way she can plausibly explain why Cat was never able to live with her mother.

In the summer Cat announces that after twenty-five years she is finally going to visit her mother in Italy. Aurélie presents her with copies of the more than two hundred letters that she has sent over the years to Charlotte which were concerned almost exclusively with Cat herself. These letters comprise an impressive record of Cat's entire life, her growing up and her relationships.

After her return from Italy, Cat tells how unsatisfactory her meeting has been with her mother, who had seemed to her to be cool and distant. She tells Aurélie that she (Aurélie) is and will remain her real mother and that even her birth mother considers her now to be Aurélie's daughter too. She has, however, given Cat a present to take back to Aurélie and the accompanying letter serves to prove that she is not as heartless and uncaring as it has seemed all those years.

This incident seems to make the already loving and deep relationship between Aurélie and Cat, simultaneously her daughter, niece and sister, even deeper than before.

Background and Commentary

Marie Laberge, the author of *Aurélie, ma sœur*, was born in 1950 in Quebec City. She studied at the Conservatoire d'Art Dramatique in her home town from 1972 till 1975 and then worked initially as an actress and later as a director and dramatist. She has written about twenty plays and several screenplays. From 1987 till 1989 she was the president of the Centre d'Essai des Auteurs Dramatiques. For the European production of *L'Homme Gris* she was awarded the *Croix de Chevalier de l'ordre des Arts et des Lettres* by the government of France.

In her plays Marie Laberge has demonstrated a special ability, through her use of diverse frameworks and convincing characters, to generate a great dramatic tension. She deals with the problems of our times both humorously and sympathetically. *Aurélie, ma sœur* was translated into English by Rina Fraticelli with the title *Sisters*. The length of the performance is approximately two hours and ten minutes.

In this two-handed play one sees two women talking about life, love, cats, flowers, sex and the awful secret that binds them together; about a person who is no longer there, whom the audience never sees and has never heard of, but who is nevertheless also a central character. The central theme of the play is the love between a young woman and her adoptive mother and their sisterly relationship which goes beyond normal familial bonds. *Aurélie, ma sœur* thematizes the sort of tenderness and affection that can heal wounds which seem to be incurable.

On stage there is very little action. The play consists solely of the conversations between Aurélie and Cat. It is concentrated on several evenings which are spread out over several years. Beneath the surface of this small talk there is a meaningful examination of reality: loyalty, secrets from the past, self-discovery and self-realisation. The contrast between Cat's ever stronger detachment from her birth mother and the continually growing relationship with her aunt determines the course of events in the play and constitutes a highly complex plot which only reveals itself toward the end of the play. One scene takes on a particular importance, namely the one in which Aurélie and Cat return from the funeral of an old man in Québec City, an old man who turns out to have been the father of both women.

Aurélie, ma sœur is not really a dramatic play. Many of the episodes, which in a film would have been filmed as separate scenes, are mentioned only in passing in the dialogue. For this reason the effect the drama has on the audience is fundamentally dependent on how well the off-stage action is made believable without letting it interfere with the action on stage. Changes in the conservatory are used to signal the passing of time. Specific demands regarding decor are specified in the text preceding the *dramatis personae*. Music by Vivaldi provides a musical backdrop for Aurélie's moods, and the positioning of the lamp, which Aurélie gives to Cat, is also very important.

Marie Laberge's play provides insights into French-speaking theatre in today's Québec. It shows that human relationships can survive in the most unexpected forms, however small-minded or bigoted the society is in which we live. Many consider *Aurélie, ma sœur* to be a political allegory, for example Michael Rutherford who wrote in the *Financial Times* on 18th October 1994 that: "One can read a political allegory into this text: either English-speaking and French-speaking Canada remains together despite all the differences between them, or Québec must press ahead with its secession." In Laberge's play—notwithstanding such political interpretations—the relationship between Aurélie and Cat is better by far than the relationship between Cat and her birth mother.

Themes
- Birth mother and adoptive mother
- Discovery and problematization of one's own origins
- Repression and coming to terms with new conditions within relationships
- Deficient/insufficient sense of responsibility (father, Pierre-Louis)

Some other plays
Available from Boréal
- *Le Faucon*
- *Pierre ou la Consolation*

Little Victories/Les Petits Pouvoirs

Suzanne Lebeau

Premiere (French): March 1982, *Théâtre Le Carrousel*, Montréal, Québec
Director: Lorraine Pintal
Premiere (English): 3rd February 1985, *Young People's Theatre*, Toronto, Ontario
Director: Richard Greenblatt
Cast: 11 (4 children, 6 parents, 1 teacher); two choruses (children, parents); possible casting of 4, 11 or more actors.
Stage Setting: Various locations, including four different homes, and also in school
Publisher/Place/Year: (Fr.) Les Éditions Leméac, Ottawa, Ontario 1983; (Eng.) Centre des Auteurs Dramatiques, Montréal, Québec 1984
Running time: 1 hour 15
Performance rights: Suzanne Lebeau, 514-529-6309, fax 514-529-6952 slebeau@vif.com

Characters

ISABELLE: 10 years old
MÈRE D'ISABELLE: 35 years old
PÈRE D'ISABELLE: 36 years old
PIERRE: 11 years old
MÈRE DE PIERRE: 30 years old

PÈRE DE PIERRE: 40 years old
MATHIEU: 9 years old
PÈRE DE MATHIEU: 33 years old
ANNE: 10 years old
MÈRE D'ANNE: 45 years old
PROFESSEUR
LE CHŒUR DES ENFANTS
LE CHŒUR DES PARENTS

Summary

The play is concerned with four children of differing temperaments and their respective parents.

In the prologue the parents' chorus chants rules of conduct for children. In turn Anne, Isabelle, Mathieu and Pierre express their contempt for such regulations and wish that people would treat them with more respect and understanding and pay more attention to what they have to say and what they need. They complain in chorus that their parents only love them when they follow their rules. For their part the parents only want "the best" for their children. Each group misunderstands the other.

The conflicts themselves are brought to light in seven scenes which represent different aspects of the course of a normal day: "Morning," "School," "Housework," "After School," "Grocery Shopping," "Supper" and "Punishment and Bedtime."

The closing scene is dominated by conciliatory tones: the parents ask their children to give them enough leisure time to allow them to deal with certain necessary things – including some things for the benefit of the children.

Background and Commentary

In the eighties and nineties *Theatre for Young Audiences* in Québec made a name for itself not only in Canada but also internationally. Theatre groups regularly perform plays for children in Montréal's Maison Théâtre and some dramatists devote themselves exclusively to youth theatre. Suzanne Lebeau is one such dramatist. She is one of the founding members of the Théâtre le Carrousel and, since 1974, has written her works almost exclusively for this theatre. The target group for her plays is children between the ages of nine and twelve years of age. Dramatists in children's theatres the world over can consider her work to be a treasure chest of material. *Petite ville deviendra grande/A City in the Making* (1981), *Une lune entre deux maisons/A Moon Between Two Houses* (1980), *La Marelle/Hopscotch* (1986), *Gil/Burt* (1990), *Contes d'enfants réels/Tales of Real Children* (1993) are but a few representative examples of her work. The performing rights of the plays are owned by the playwright herself.

Les Petits Pouvoirs was translated in 1983 by Maureen LaBonté into English with the title *Little Victories*. The central subject of this play is the family as the setting of constant arguments and disputes. Four children between nine and twelve and three sets of parents are the main figures in this play. Additional characters are the *Professeur* and the two choruses. All the action takes place on a single day.

The protagonists, Anne, Isabelle, Mathieu and Pierre are very much against their parents' orders; they demand more understanding for their needs and problems. In school their natural exuberance is necessarily suppressed and at other times of the day they hardly have any opportunities to do the things that they would really like to do.

Les Petits Pouvoirs is a plea for more communication between parents and children, also that childhood and growing up be understood for what they really are; as part of the reality of life in all manner of different or possible forms. The play itself is a result of extensive research into the wishes and desires of children and the reality of their lives. Lebeau collected together different experiences in her initial workshops: parents, school and money are decisive and inextricable triggers of stress among children between the ages of nine and thirteen. In later workshops the children were encouraged to figure out what sort of things led to tension or aggression (however irrelevant they might seem to be) in order to limit deterioration in their relationships. The family situation turned out to be a very sensitive area. The emotional burden carried by intra-familial relationships can have grave consequences. Each member of the group at the workshop examined everyday situations in great detail in order to understand the mechanisms that cause tension. *Les Petits Pouvoirs*, however, does not pretend to give us the answers, rather, as Dominique Demers wrote in *Le Devoir*:

> *Les Petits Pouvoirs* ne se présente pas non plus comme une pièce à recettes et messages. […] Suzanne Lebeau ne suggère même pas un remède ou un arbitrage. Elle se contente, à la toute fin du spectacle, d'illustrer une trève. (*Le Devoir*, 23rd March 1985)

Lebeau's many years of experience in the theatre and in teaching clearly find their expression in *Les Petits Pouvoirs*. She was educated in Montréal; she studied under Ètienne Decroux in Paris and completed a one-year apprenticeship in Poland. Many of her plays have been translated into different languages and have been performed worldwide.

Themes
- Misunderstandings between parents and children
- The desire for more respect
- Children's need for independence
- Social pressures and norms

Some other plays

- *La Marelle* (Leméac Éditeur)
  Hopscotch – translated by Maureen La Bonté (Carrousel Theatre)
  Target audience: Ages 4 to 7
- *Comment Vivre avec les hommes quand on est un géant* (Leméac Éditeur)
  A Giant in the Land of Man – translated by Shelley Tepperman
  (Commissioned by Prairie Theatre Exchange, Winnipeg)
  Target audience: children ages 8 to 12 and family audiences
- *Conte du jour et de la nuit* (Leméac Éditeur)
  A Tale of Day and Night – translated by John Van Burek (first produced
  by Carrousel Theatre)
  Target audience: Ages 4 to 8
- *Salvador la montagne, l'enfant et la mangue* (VLB Éditeur)
  Salvador: the Mountain, the Mango and the Child – translated by John
  Van Burek (first produced by Carrousel Theatre)
  Target audience: Age 8 and up

Sisters

Wendy Lill

Premiere: August 1989, *Ship's Company Theatre*, Parrsboro, Nova Scotia
Director: Mary Vingoe
Cast: 6 (4 women and 2 men)
Stage Setting: Various locations including a custody cell in rural Nova Scotia (1969); a nearby farm (1950); a boarding school for Indians (50s and 60s)
Publisher/Place/Year: Talonbooks, Vancouver, British Columbia 1991
Length: 95 pages
Performance Rights: Patricia Ney, Christopher Banks & Associates, 6 Adelaide St. E., Ste. 610, Toronto, Ontario M5C 1H6, 416-214-1155, fax 416-214-1150

Characters
YOUNG MARY
LOUIS
GABRIEL
AGNES
MARY
STEIN

Summary

Mary, a forty-one-year-old nun, is arrested for arson. Her lawyer, Stein, seeks to find out her motives, but Mary remains, for the time being, uncommunicative. Her thoughts keep returning to her past. At one time she reminisces about the time when she was seventeen and was with her boyfriend Louis. Then she thinks about the time when she first taught, as a nun, and worked together in a school for Native children with Sister Gabriel and Mother Agnes. From time to time when Mary's memories and feelings become particularly intense, the three plot levels seem to merge together.

Her aversion to speaking is partly linked to the fact that because of her isolated life as a nun she is not at all used to speaking about her private life. It is also because she finds it difficult to admit to herself what her motives were. Because of her reticence Stein dominates their conversations with tales from his own life, a life which has been very frustrating because he has still not achieved the "Star Lawyer" status that he covets so much.

Whenever Stein starts believing that he is never going to bring Mary out of her shell, he makes a move to go. Yet Mary repeatedly prevents him from going. It is not until the end that she finally tells him why she burned down the school where she has taught Native children for fifteen years. It is because she became a nun to love other people and to do good works, but convent life with its strict rules has ruined her and her life. It has driven her to destroy the very thing which destroyed her life and the lives of many others.

By means of the various levels of action, both temporal and geographical, which provide a backdrop for Mary's reminiscences, the play reconstructs Mary's development from a warm-hearted young idealist into a person who follows the rules of the convent and the school without consideration for her own feelings.

Background and Commentary

Sisters is a blunt examination of the practices in a convent school for Canadian Native children. Yet the play is much more than a criticism of the sterile atmosphere and the unsparingly hard regulations in some Catholic schools in Canada where the sisters are often just as oppressed as the pupils themselves. It questions this whole concept of education. The play itself is not based on actual events, but cases of corruption in schools, however, such as Mount Cashel in Newfoundland, a film of which has been shown on television screens as far away as Germany and is also well-known from newspaper reports.

The central figure in *Sisters* is Sister Mary, a nun who has taught Native children in a boarding school for fifteen years. The play is a shocking but moving portrait of an individual who finds herself within an overpowering infrastructure which permits no questioning of its motives and where dreams are nipped in the bud. *Sisters* is a passionately and honestly written play which challenges the audience by showing them the necessity of never avoiding uncomfortable questions and of not shrinking away from confrontations with unpleasant answers.

Wendy Lill was born in Vancouver and was educated in London, Ontario and Toronto. She lived for many years in Winnipeg and now lives with her family in Dartmouth, Nova Scotia. She is currently a Member of Parliament in Canada's House of Commons, and is the Culture and People With Disabilities critic for the New Democratic Party (NDP).

Sisters received the *Labatt's Canadian Play Award* at the Newfoundland and Labrador Drama Festival. Primedia Productions brought out a television version of the play which Lill scripted.

Themes
- Appearance and reality of convent life
- Minority problems
- Overvaluation of the dominant culture
- Consequences of an alienated and perverted Christianity

Some other plays
Available from Playwrights Guild of Canada:
- *The Occupation of Heather Rose*

Available from Talonbooks:
- *All Fall Down*
- *Corker*
- *The Fighting Days*
- *Glace Bay Miners' Museum*
- *Memories of You*

Goodnight Desdemona (Good Morning Juliet)

Ann-Marie MacDonald

Premiere: 1988, *Annex Theatre*, Toronto, Ontario; production by *Nightwood Theatre*

Director: Banuta Rubess

Cast: 15 (6 women, 9 men) and a chorus

Stage Setting: Various locations: A bedroom, a university office, a citadel at Cyprus; a public place in Verona, Capulet Hall, a balcony overlooking an orchard, the boneyard, a crypt

Publisher/Place/Year: Coach House Press, Toronto, Ontario 1990; Vintage Press. Toronto, Ontario 1998

Length: 87 pages

Performance rights: Lorraine Wells & Company, 10 St. Mary St., Ste. 320, Toronto, Ontario M4Y 1P9, 416-413-1676, fax 416-413-1680

Characters

DESDEMONA	OTHELLO
JULIET	ROMEO
IAGO	CHORUS
TYBALT	MERCUTIO
A SOLDIER OF CYPRUS	JULIET'S NURSE
SERVANT	GHOST

CONSTANCE LEDBELLY: an assistant professor at Queen's University

STUDENT: "Julie, uh Jill", a student at Queen's University

RAMONA: a student at Queen's University

PROFESSOR CLAUDE NIGHT: university professor, boss to Constance Ledbelly

Summary

Constance Ledbelly, a lecturer in Renaissance drama at Queen's University, is drifting into non-existence. Her beauty is slowly fading and her intellect is being stifled. Her dream is to win the recognition that she deserves by deciphering the mysterious Gustav manuscript which, she claims, contains the original texts for Shakespeare's *Othello* and *Romeo & Juliet*. But her intellect is being stolen by the oily Professor Night, all of whose papers she is forced to ghost-write, and her beauty is being stolen by time itself. As she realizes she is being "phased out" in favour of a younger model, namely the much younger Ramona, she begins to despair.

At this point Constance realizes she has the chance to prove her theory that Shakespeare's two tragedies were in fact comedies with the fool simply removed. She must solve the riddle of the fool to prove her thesis and embarks on a quest to find the missing pages which will reveal the name of the Author. Entering Othello's world she quickly alters the story, as we know it from Shakespeare, dramatically, by foiling Iago's plan to discredit Desdemona—as she had surmised the fool in the original text must have done—she saves Desdemona's life. But he unwittingly becomes the source of Othello's affections and Iago now plots to discredit Constance. During this time Constance notes that she has lapsed into blank verse, speaking the same unrhymed iambic pentameter as the characters around her, who speak a mixture of authentic Shakespearean dialogue and original lines.

Just as the situation in Cyprus becomes extremely precarious for Constance she is again whisked away, this time to Verona where she arrives just in time to stop Romeo's fatal intervention in Mercutio's and Tybalt's duel. In Verona she is mistaken by the other characters for a boy, Constantine. Again she intervenes in the plot and not only becomes the subject of Romeo's affections but also of Juliet's! Here the amusing dialogue and comic asides become more and more closely packed as the tragedy does indeed become a farcical comedy. And for a while the play proceeds like a comedy of errors.

Then, following an amusing encounter with a ghost (the chorus in disguise) whose dialogue comes straight from Groucho Marx, Constance receives her final clue. She must unite the trinity of herself, Juliet and Desdemona to solve the riddle. In the final scenes she achieves this aim and the ghost reveals that she herself is the Wise Fool, the Author of the story whereupon she is transported back to the halls of academe.

Background and commentary

The idea to the play came up during a tour of England in 1985 when Ann-Marie MacDonald playfully threw a pillow at Banuta Rubess and shouted "Goodnight Desdemona."

MacDonald was born on a Royal Air Force Base in Baden-Baden,

West Germany, in 1958. Her father was of Scottish and her mother of Lebanese ancestry, but Cape Breton was to become her home. Fairly early on, she went to live in Montréal and to train at the National Theatre School, from which she graduated in 1980. Before she got the idea for her first solo writing venture, MacDonald had collaborated with Beverly Cooper and had taken part in a theatre project (*This is for You, Anna*). But *Goodnight Desdemona* was to become her breakthrough as a playwright. As in her other ventures before and in *The Arab's Mouth* later on, feminism and her own sexuality as a lesbian were of significant influence on the play, which skilfully turns the ideas of gender into their opposites to explore Constance's character and sexuality. Desdemona and Juliet represent the two poles of Constance's self between which she seems to be drawn all the time. Romeo's latent homosexuality is only a by-effect of the complex plot, not vital but presenting a nuance that should not be missed.

This parody of Shakespeare challenges the traditional rules of poetic realism as Marc Maufort has pointed out (see also Maufort, Marc. "Poetic Realism reinvented: Canadian Women Playwrights and the Search for a New Theatrical Idiom." In: *Canadian Studies* 42. Bordeaux, 1997), but it does so with a light humour that illuminates Constance's troubles while at the same time protecting the character from corruption.

Ann-Marie MacDonald not only received the Chalmers Award for Outstanding Drama (1988) for *Goodnight Desdemona* but also the 1990 Governor General's Award for Drama. As demonstrated by *The Totally Portable Theatre Company* at the Grace Theatre, London, in 1997, the play can be put on stage with minimal set and props, and actors can comfortably play several roles. Nevertheless, the length of the text should be taken into account: Constance alone has more lines than Hamlet.

The playwright herself has never played in her own work as she wants to distance herself from it once it is written. She thinks the companies should make the play their own.

Themes
- Classical foils used for feminist reappraisals
- Familiar characters in unfamiliar environments
- Two worlds turning from tragedy to comedy
- How to keep control over one's life.

Some other plays
Available from Playwrights Guild of Canada:
- *Clue in the Fast Lane*
- *Nigredo Hotel*

Available from Scirocco Drama:
- *The Attic, the Pearls, and Three Fine Girls*

House

Daniel
MacIvor

Premiere: May 1992, *Factory Theatre Studio Café*, Toronto, Ontario; pro-
duced by *Da Da Kamera* in association with the *Factory Theatre*
Director: Daniel Brooks
Cast: 1 man
Stage Setting: Empty stage
Publisher/Place/Year: In: *House Humans*, Coach House Press, Toronto,
Ontario 1992; Playwrights Canada Press, Toronto, Ontario 1996
Length: 47 pages
Performance Rights: Daniel MacIvor Inc., Da Da Kamera, 401 Richmond
St. W., Toronto, Ontario M5V 3A8, 416-586-1503, fax 416-586-1504

Character
VICTOR

Summary
    House is a monodrama. The character of Victor functions more as a
narrator than as an actor playing a role. He recounts episodes from his life,
a life that he is less than happy with.
    He has worked for twelve years in the offices of a company which
supplies septic tanks, although he had really wanted to become an engi-
neer. In this, however, he was unlucky, as in many other things in his life.
He is married to MaryAnn, his third cousin. He loves her, but she does not
love him and betrays him finally with his boss who has never really taken

Victor seriously. This hurts Victor very much. MaryAnn, who is of a some-what perverse disposition, ends the relationship. What's more, Victor's boss wants to buy Victor's house so in the end Victor is left with nothing. He cannot rely on his family as his parents are particularly stubborn and his sister has an abnormal relationship with her dog.

The only support Victor receives is from his therapy group, which he admittedly doesn't think much of, but which he regularly visits, and also in his chaotic daydreams which transport him into other worlds.

It is with one of these daydreams that the play ends; a dream in which Victor travels by bus to Wadawhichawawa. Suddenly all the bus passengers begin to sing a song about a man who wants to build a house for his beloved so that they can live happily ever after.

Background and Commentary

One man stands alone on the stage, his bony face thrown into sharp relief by the harsh light of a spotlight. He grabs a stool and hurls it madly around the stage. He does this repeatedly until finally he sits and thanks the audience for coming and not staying at home in front of the television. All this takes place at the beginning of a play which has no real plot, as such. In a one-hour monologue the man tells stories from his unsatisfac-tory life. He tells of his father, who appeared on posters as the "saddest man in the world;" of his mother, who is possessed by the devil; of his wife, who is unfaithful to him; of his sister, who dances with dogs. These stories or anecdotes all have one thing in common: they all accentuate his isola-tion and confusion. He is a loser and transforms his world into a landscape of madness.

Victor (what an ironic name!) is the man's name and he is utterly at home in the world of fast food, telephone sex and group therapy. But it is only through the last of these that he finds contact with other people: peo-ple, however, that he either hates or envies. However, he considers the $12,000 that he spends on renovating his house, just because his boss is coming to dinner, to be worth it.

Victor is a homeowner without a spiritual home. His spirit swings between fear, fury and grovelling. "What the hell is the matter with me?" he seems to be asking as a representative of many people in the Western "civilised" world.

Victor's way of talking does a lot to reveal the state of his psyche. He can only partly articulate what he really wants to say. He often repeats the same sentence over and over – albeit with a few minor variations. He fre-quently loses his thread and tries to find it again using word associations which then spark off the aforementioned anecdotes. In terms of structure, *House* is a mosaic of improvised reflections about love and lost love, suc-cess and failure and about the role of group therapy in the life of a seeker. Originally the play was not scripted, it was worked out in 1992 in a workshop. Daniel MacIvor played the role of Victor himself. *House* received the Chalmers Award for best play of 1992.

As an actor MacIvor worked in films but originally he studied journalism at Dalhousie University. His best known works include: *Never Swim Alone*, *2-2 Tango*, *See Bob Run* and *Wild Abandon*. Like *House*, all these plays are relatively short, with performance times rarely over sixty minutes. MacIvor laconically observes that because people today are not especially motivated to go to the theatre one cannot afford to take too much of their time.

Themes
- Mental disorientation
- Isolation and loneliness
- Love and the loss of love
- The search for one's own self

Some other plays
Available from Playwrights Canada Press:
- *2-2 Tango* (in *Making, Out*)
- *Here Lies Henry*
- *House Humans*
- *Never Swim Alone & This is a Play* (two plays)
- *See Bob Run & Wild Abandon* (two plays)
- *Theatre Omaha's Production of The Sound of Music*

Available from Scirocco:
- *Monster*
- *The Soldier Dreams*
- *You Are Here*

Available from Talonbooks:
- *Marion Bridge*

Toronto, Mississippi

Joan MacLeod

Premiere: 6th October 1987, *Tarragon Theatre*, Toronto, Ontario
Director: Andy McKim
Cast: 4 (2 women, 2 men)
Stage Setting: Middle-class living room in Toronto, Ontario
Publisher/Place/Year: In: *Toronto, Mississippi & Jewel*, Playwrights Canada Press, Toronto, Ontario 1987
Length: 104 pages
Performance rights: Patricia Ney, Christopher Banks & Associates, 6 Adelaide St. E., Ste. 610, Toronto, Ontario M5C 1H6, 416-214-1155, fax 416-214-1150

Characters

KING: 40 years old; Jhana's father; Elvis impersonator
JHANA: 18 years old; moderately mentally handicapped; works in a sheltered workshop
BILL: 30 years old; lodges with Maddie and Jhana; poet and part-time lecturer
MADDIE: 40 years old; Jhana's mother; English teacher in a high school

Summary

Maddie's, Jhana's and their lodger Bill's lives are all thrown into confusion when Maddie's estranged husband suddenly appears. Jhana is extremely fond of her father. Maddie and King's relationship is complicated: she knows how unreliable and unhelpful her husband is but is nevertheless unwilling to completely let go of him. King's unexpected appearance leaves her feeling confronted by the question as to who she really is and whether she is not perhaps too protective of Jhana having made all her decisions for her for such a long time.

When King decides to stay a couple of days longer, Maddie feels caught somewhere between the two men. Bill is not just her best friend but he is also someone who Jhana can relate to. He shows no small interest in having a relationship with Maddie.

The tense atmosphere erupts when King sees Bill kissing Jhana and knocks him to the floor. Maddie arrives and throws King out of the house – this time for good. But the questions that King's appearance has driven to the surface remain unanswered. All those concerned are left to consider things a bit more deeply.

Background and Commentary

Toronto, Mississippi, premiered at the Tarragon Theatre in Toronto in 1987, is a play ostensibly about Jhana Gladys Kelly, a likeable girl whose autism, learning difficulties and hyperactivity present her with considerable difficulties. The author, Joan MacLeod, worked with young people with similar problems in Vancouver while she was there studying creative writing. The inspiration for this play came from one girl in particular who she had got to know at that time and whose development between the ages of ten and twenty-one she was able to see first-hand. The focus of this play, however, is not exclusively on the young girl and her relationship to those people in her immediate vicinity. It also falls on the character of Maddie, a forty-year-old teacher, who tries to combine her desire to lead an independent life with her concern with her daughter's welfare. It also falls on Bill, a college instructor who wants to be thought of as a poet although he has only ever published a very slim volume of work. He is sexually frustrated and self-pitying and is also a kind of ersatz father to Jhana. Occasionally he shows a great deal of affection to Jhana which she ultimately does not reciprocate. Jhana's father left years ago; he adores his daughter but is unwilling to take on responsibility for her. He is an Elvis impersonator by trade; for this reason he has taken on the name King. He is Jhana's idol and she also attempts to sing Elvis' songs. From time to time she identifies with her father, then with herself and then with a dead man. She confuses Tupelo, Mississippi, Elvis' birthplace, with Toronto – hence the title of the play.

Toronto, Mississippi follows the development of the relationships between four people which leads to a dramatic conflict when King suddenly turns up. But it is Jhana who is really the catalyst; she is a mirror in which the good and bad characteristics of the people around her are made visible.

Gord McCall, who chose *Toronto, Mississippi* for his directorial debut in Sudbury, described his choice in the journal *Northern Life* (14th April 1991) in the following way:

> This play represents much of what I like in theatre – an excellent story, compelling characters, plenty of humour, strong emotions and a powerful blend of theatricality and moving human drama.

What seems on the surface to be a relatively simple story (Bill loves Maddie who loves King and everyone loves Jhana) turns out to be an emotionally loaded tangle of relationships which has been put together thoughtfully and realistically. The subplots—the animosity between the two "artists," Bill and King, also Bill's desire for Maddie set against Maddie's continuing desire to share the marital bed with her inconstant, unreliable husband, King, and finally Jhana's awakening sexuality—are all subordinated to the central events. The particular quality of the play lies in the fact that we see the relationships between the central characters to a great extent from Jhana's unique perspective.

Toronto, Mississippi contains dramatically explosive material. It raises important issues about the conceptions of men's and women's roles, about pop culture and its effects on behaviour patterns of people today. Above all *Toronto, Mississippi* makes an important contribution to the debate about the problem(s) of disability (one thinks also of Peter Nichols' *A Day in the Life of Joe Egg*). Some critics have also interpreted MacLeod's play as a symbolic representation of the (not always harmonic) relationship between the United States and Canada.

Themes
- The problems of disability (autism, learning difficulties)
- Coming to terms with relationships
- Unrequited love
- Defining the role of man and woman
- Pop culture and idols

Some other plays
Available from Playwrights Canada Press:
- *Toronto, Mississippi & Jewel* (two plays)

Available from Talonbooks:
- *Amigo's Blue Guitar*
- *The Hope Slide & Little Sister* (two plays)
- *Shape of a Girl*
- *2000*

Possible Worlds

John Mighton

Premiere: November 1990, *St. Lawrence Centre*, Toronto, Ontario; pro-
  duction by *Canadian Stage Company*
Director: Peter Hinton
Cast: 5 (1 woman, 4 men)
Stage Setting: A bachelor apartment, various rooms and offices
Publisher/Place/Year: Playwrights Canada Press, Toronto, Ontario 1998
Length: 70 pages
Performance Rights: Sherrie Johnson, Da Da Kamera, 401 Richmond St.
  W., Toronto, Ontario M5V 3A8, 416-586-1503, fax 416-586-1504

Characters
GEORGE: between 20 and 30 years old
JOYCE: between 20 and 30 years old
BERKLEY: a detective
WILLIAMS: Berkley's assistant
PENFIELD: a neurologist

Summary
   A psychopathic murderer is going round and stealing the brains of
his victims. One finds out at the end that one of these belongs to George
Barber. Concurrent to the police investigations George finds himself in an
alternative world where he meets a woman called Joyce. The two have
many encounters and each of these meetings runs slightly differently to

the previous one. George remembers each of the previous meetings whereas Joyce meets George each time for the first time. Their relationship becomes increasingly intense. The first time they meet Joyce gives George the brush-off, the next time she is more interested, later they are in a "proper" relationship, then Joyce leaves for a while, but in the final scene they are reunited and this time apparently forever ("Where will we go?" – "Everywhere"[1]).

In the penultimate scene it becomes clear that George has been dead for some time and that Joyce is actually George's wife, who, in his parallel universe, he thinks is dead.

There is no solution. But the suspicion is that in the real world, in other words that of the police and the audience, Joyce is alive and George is dead. His brain, however, is still alive and he travels through numerous "possible worlds" looking for Joyce. Here there is one real world and many fantasy worlds, yet the play on reality and the question as to how far reality and fantasy are separate allows many other interpretations.

Background and Commentary

The central question of John Mighton's *Possible Worlds* is: what is it that makes a human being the individual that he or she really is and—despite all spatial and temporal changes—remains? The main theme is, therefore, a person's inner identity; the action takes place in the present.

The author uses parallel stories to speculate over the existence of parallel worlds. What you have, according to Mighton, is only relative to what you are able to imagine. Mighton's pronounced interest in the question of identity and parallel worlds, which shows clear signs of the influence of Wittgenstein and Nietzsche, grew out of a four-year stay in New York in the early eighties and during the period of his study of philosophy and (later) mathematics and physics at the University of Toronto. He is the youngest of six children of a doctor in Hamilton, Ontario.

In New York he lived in the Lower East Side, at the time still a no-man's land and a haven for drug dealers, squatters and crazy people who opened art galleries. Mighton was aware of all these different people and believed they would make good subject matter for his plays which would be characterised by absurd events yet were based on reality. At that time he did actually write four short dramas.

Possible Worlds has its roots in the research done by American scientists in the fifties who came to the conclusion that separation of parts of the brain stem could effectively hinder attacks of epilepsy. From this arose the philosophical question: if one were to transplant one half of a human brain with all its memories and dispositions into another person which of the two individuals would then count as the "original" person? What is it

---

[1] Page 78, *Possible Worlds & A Short History of Night*, John Mighton, Playwrights Canada Press 1992

that keeps a person being the same person his whole life? How could the world perhaps be different? Physicists talk of parallel universes, other scientists construct models of economically or ecologically better worlds and philosophers imagine alternative worlds.

Mighton picked up on the idea that both halves of the brain could continue to function with independent consciousness even after they had been physically disconnected from each other. He distanced himself from the idea that one half of the brain was responsible for speech and logic and the other for creativity, emotion and fantasy. *Possible Worlds*, his imaginative "what if" drama, resists the conventional either/or rational versus emotional idea, which says that a mathematician cannot be an artist and an artist cannot be a mathematician at the same time. This assumed separation is a twentieth century idea. Indeed his work with "underachievers," that is to say those people who had no confidence in their ability to understand mathematical and physical relationships, was a strong influence on him and raised the question for him whether such a thing as natural or innate intelligence even exists.

In interviews the author frequently makes reference to the fact that Shakespeare and the metaphysical poets frequently borrowed concepts from scientists for their metaphors. For them there was no boundary between reason and emotion, between head and heart. Mighton himself called upon the metaphor of many conceivable worlds in order to sound out human potential and to shed light on the grey zone between identity and imagination, between real and imagined worlds.

One might expect from this explanation that *Possible Worlds* was a dry and abstract piece, which despite its interesting content would not work too well on stage because it is too theoretical and conceptual. This is not at all the case. The action is spiced with irony, humour and absurdity and, in a second thread of the plot, carries traits of a dramatised detective story. While Joyce and George, a young pair to begin with, meet in a café, then in a bar, then on the beach in one line of the plot, in the other one meets a detective on the trail of a serial killer who steals the brains of his victims. Joyce and George are joined in a peculiar kind of romance, and though Joyce lives in two parallel worlds—she is a neurologist yet also a financial broker—George seems to have no problem with that because he also lives in different possible worlds. The detective discovers the brain of the murdered man which has been kept alive as part of a scientific experiment. "He's still alive… we found his brain… in a cupboard… hooked up to a life support system,"[2] says the detective to Joyce, and then later asks, "What would you like me to do with the brain when it stops functioning?"

---

[2] Page 71. *Possible Worlds & A Short History of Night*, John Mighton, Playwrights Canada Press 1992

And she replies, "Donate it to science."[3] Various comic-grotesque moments in the play give the piece its "bizarre comic book aspect" as one critic put it.

The end of the detective story is not perhaps what one might expect. There are no trails or suspected "alternative worlds" that turn out to be false because the correct solution has been crystallised out of the clues. Mighton's play is ambiguous. "There are different conceivable explanations for what has happened," says the author, and "We want to know what it is that makes a person what he is. But such questions are so far beyond our intelligence that any attempt to answer them seems a little comical." It is probably true that many Canadians consider their own world in fairly ironic terms. They have the tendency to make wry comments about ambitious ideas and grandiose events.

Themes
• Man as an individual
• The relationship of reality to imagination
• The two halves of the human brain
• Rational and emotional – an either/or question?
• Qualification of human identity

Some other plays
Available from Playwrights Canada Press:
• *Body & Soul*
• *The Little Years*
• *Scientific Americans*
• *A Short History of Night*

Available from Playwrights Guild of Canada:
• *A Short History of Night*

[3] Page 72. *Possible Worlds & A Short History of Night*, John Mighton, Playwrights Canada Press 1992

Almighty Voice and His Wife

Daniel David Moses

Premiere: 20th September 1991, *Great Canadian Theatre Company*, Ottawa, Ontario

Director: Lib Spry

Cast: 2 (1 woman, 1 man)

Stage Setting: The Saskatchewan prairie; on the auditorium stage of an abandoned school

Publisher/Place/Year: Williams-Wallace Publishers, Stratford, Ontario 1992; Playwrights Canada Press, Toronto, Ontario 2001

Length: 97 pages

Performance rights: Patricia Ney, Christopher Banks & Associates, 6 Adelaide St. E., Ste. 610, Toronto, Ontario M5C 1H6, 416-214-1155, fax 416-214-1150

Characters

ALMIGHTY VOICE: in act one, a young Cree in his mid-twenties; later a ghost
WHITE GIRL: in act one a young Cree teenager; Almighty Voice's wife; in act two the INTERLOCUTOR

Summary

Canada in the 19th century. Almighty Voice woos the intelligent and practically-minded White Girl who has been brought up in a white school. White Girl is aware that the future looks pretty bleak for the Indian people and tries every possible trick she knows to protect Almighty Voice from the gods and from men. But he is young and proud and although he knows that the police are after him he shoots a Mountie and has to flee. White Girl—already carrying his child—stays at home not wanting to be a burden to him. Far away, at a deserted spot, he is shot. As he dies he sees his newborn son in a vision.

Act Two begins with an Indian show with dancing, singing and stories. The ghost of Almighty Voice is the only performer. At first he only reluctantly tells his story whilst performing a few dance steps. Gradually, however, he begins to take control of events drawing the interlocutor ever more into the show and lets him tell the story. In this way the interlocutor loses his whiteness, transforms himself into an Indian and finally becomes White Girl. While Almighty Voice's ghost dances one last dance under the fading stage lights, White Girl removes her white makeup and her Mountie costume and holding her baby aloft presents herself to the audience as an Indian.

Background and Commentary

Daniel David Moses is a Delaware Indian from the Six Nations Lands in southern Ontario. He has lived for many years in Toronto. Further Moses plays include *Coyote City*, *Big Buck City* and *The Dreaming Beauty*.

Almighty Voice and his Wife, written in 1991, is based on a story, well-known to many Canadian Natives, which Moses only came across in the early eighties. The popular version concerns a mischievous young Indian who was taken into police custody in 1895 for shooting a cow. While he was there someone jokingly told him that the penalty for killing a cow was hanging and the young man fled in fear of his life. When a policeman finally tracked him down he didn't give himself up but instead, in fear of the rope, shot the policeman. From then on he was considered an outlaw and in the company of two accomplices managed to escape the law for the next one-and-a-half years. His wife was also with him for a while. Finally, however, the three men fell into a police trap and, despite killing one of the policemen, were themselves killed by the arriving cavalry. No one knows where the men were buried.

At that time Almighty Voice lived in Saskatchewan, one of the first generation of Natives who had been forced to live on the reserves and who rebelled against these measures and against the impending destruction of their culture.

Daniel David Moses added another dimension to this story by adding White Girl, Almighty Voice's wife, into the equation. The play consists of two acts. The first act tells the story of the two young people. At the beginning Almighty Voice is nineteen and White Girl is twelve. White Girl's odyssey is the central theme of the second act. She is forced to go to a school run by white people and is confronted by Christian thought and the white people's lifestyle. Very soon she runs the risk of having her Native origins subsumed by this new culture.

What is also important to Moses in this play is the presentation of the love story between Almighty Voice and White Girl. This finds its expression, however, only in small vignettes, which are made subordinate to the other plot lines which, for their own part, fit together to portray the slow extinction of Native culture by the white people.

The form and message of this play may be nothing new but the dramatic conception is quite original. The staging of the somewhat long-winded first act requires modern performance techniques as nine short scenes have to present nine short episodes from the lives of the two protagonists. Soon dance, rhythmic singing and drumming fill in the gaps in the text; then come more dialogues, longer speeches or short statements. Many critics in Canada went so far as to describe the first act as a transformation of the lives of Almighty Voice and White Girl into legend. The presentation does indeed leave everyday reality far behind and avoids being lost in clichés.

The second act is a strong attack on "white" culture in the form of a sort of American "minstrel" show which serves as a metaphor for the mainstream culture and its attitude towards Natives. The two Indian figures from the first act now appear as clowns. White Girl, her face painted, now plays a man; an embodiment of the powers that are destroying Native culture. Daniel David Moses clearly very carefully researched the minstrel show and then deliberately turned its focus around in the other direction. While in minstrel shows white performers coloured their faces with black makeup and then to the delight of their white audiences tastelessly parodied Black people, in *Almighty Voice and his Wife* White Girl appears as a white master of ceremonies and laughing and dancing proceeds to bring in all the popular clichés about Natives.

As the Ghost, however, Almighty Voice is a caricature of himself. White Girl (here a white man) in the role of the Interlocutor makes him dance and ridicules him while he is trying to recount how he met his death.

By means of the jump in time and the thus unavoidable break between the two parts of the play and their accompanying shift in style, and also by means of the end where Almighty Voice and his wife metamorphose back into their original characters, Daniel David Moses manages to achieve a reaction from the audience which is somewhat akin to the shock felt by the Natives during colonisation. *Almighty Voice and his Wife* clearly brings home (as an example of how Natives were treated by the white man) what the lack of readiness to understand other lifestyles and the hanging onto of non-representative racial stereotypes can bring about in relation to different cultures (see also the section on *Fronteras Americanas* by Guillermo Verdecchia in this book). Mira Friedlander quoted Moses' own comments in her article in *The Toronto Star*:

> I wanted to look at human values that have taken hundreds of thousands of years to develop into a society, only to be ripped apart in one century by an economic system that works to isolate people and turn everyone into a good consumer. (*The Toronto Star*, 7th February 1992)

Themes
- The Indian conception of self
- Treatment of Natives by colonists
- The role of Native women
- Rebellion against oppression
- Alienation and stereotypes

Some other plays
Available from Playwrights Guild of Canada:
- *Big Buck City*
- *Brebeuf's Ghost*
- *The Dreaming Beauty*
- *The Witch of Niagara*

Available from Exile Editions:
- *The Moon and Dead Indians* (in *Indian Medicine Shows*)

Available from Imago Press:
- *Coyote City & City of Shadows* (two titles)

Farther West

John Murrell

Premiere: 22nd April 1982, *Theatre Calgary*, Calgary, Alberta
Director: Robin Phillips
Cast: 11 (4 women, 7 men)
Stage Setting: Various settings in Ontario, British Columbia and the Northwest Territories between 1886 and 1892
Publisher/Place/Year: In: *Farther West, New World. Two Plays by John Murrell*, Coach House Press, Toronto, Ontario 1985
Length: 82 pages
Performance rights: Playwrights Canada Press or murrellj@nucleus.com

Characters
MAY BUCHANAN
A MAN IN BED WITH HER
THOMAS SHEPHERD
SEWARD
VIOLET DECARMIN
NETTIE MCDOWELL
LILY REEVES
BABCOCK
ROSS
RAGLAN
HANKS

Summary

At the tender age of fourteen May is thrown out of her home by her father for sleeping with men for money. Thereupon she finds herself on an uncertain journey westwards because her father has told her that in the west there is a place where there are no morals.

In the summer of 1888 she meets Violet, another woman who earns her money in the "oldest trade," in Calgary. May quickly becomes the madame of a bordello where she works together with Violet, Lily and Nettie. Ross, the assistant of the puritanical Seward, arrests May for keeping a "disorderly house" after exposing her through trickery. She, however, uses her feminine wiles on Seward to get out of jail.

Another attempt by Seward to arrest May, when he catches her in the open with Thomas Shepherd, fails when she flees with him. Shepherd is in love with May and wants to marry her. Seward is also strongly attracted to her despite his moral objections.

For nine months May lives with Shepherd in the Northwest Territories. However, in the summer of 1891 her yearning for freedom drives her westwards once more. In a fight where Shepherd tries to prevent May from leaving, she shoots him in the shoulder and flees once more.

Later, in the winter of the same year, May is back together with Violet working as a whore in Vancouver. It is not too long, however, before Shepherd tracks her down again and demands that she go with him. In the argument that follows, May reaches for his pistol but Shepherd manages to wrest it from her. His senses somewhat fuddled by alcohol and desperation, he shoots her. Mary feigns death and while he mourns for her she shoots him dead.

But May is also badly injured. She makes Violet take her to the harbour, which for her is a symbol of freedom. She is found there by Seward, who in the meantime has been suspended from the police force because of his fanatical pursuit of May. He is, however, still possessed by the idea of arresting her. Yet when he aims his pistol at May—despite Violet's attempts to hold him back—he quickly realises that she is already dead. He shoves the boat in which she is lying into the water and finally gives her the freedom that she has sought so long.

Background and Commentary

John Murrell, the author of *Farther West*, was born in the United States but has lived for many years in Calgary. As early as the seventies, Murrell had developed a close relationship with the theatre of the region. His milieu is the prairie but his plays are performed all over the world. This applies especially to *Memoir* (1978) a play about Sarah Bernhardt's last summer that has been translated into a dozen languages and has been enthusiastically received in Europe and South America.

Farther West is an epic piece about a prostitute from Calgary who is looking for independence and self-determination. It is very loosely based on a real story of a prostitute who left Ontario and made her way via Calgary and the Northwest Territories to Vancouver and the pacific coast where she died in 1892.

In *Farther West* Murrell leaves behind many of the characteristic European perspectives, such as one finds in many of his other plays, and instead turns his attention to the mythical and moralistic aspects of life in the Canadian west. May Buchanan is the name of the prostitute and "Go west!" is her motto. The search for her own identity takes her ever further west and although she sometimes has cause to doubt herself, she never questions the motives of her lifestyle. She makes full use of the opportunities that are presented to her as she continues west to test the range of her identity. Who am I? and Who could I be? These questions accompany her every step of the way. (Was Murrell thinking perhaps of Sarah Bernhardt?) In *Farther West* Seward symbolises the authority and traditional moral values in the 19th century which have given way to the doubts of the 20th century.

"Next?" is May's first comment in Murrell's play: what—or perhaps rather who—comes next? "Next" becomes a *leitmotif* in May's life. She wants to leave the past behind but every present for her—in the search for an uncertain future—quickly becomes a past. Her "going west," which for her symbolises her freedom and independence, leads her eventually to the shocking scenes of violence and eventually murder. At the end of *Farther West* one is left with the moving image of May's body lying in a rowing boat floating out into the water – farther west into the ocean.

What particularly characterises this play is the richly-facetted language, and the successful combination of pictures and music and songs which underline the action. Further plays from Murrell include: *Waiting for the Parade* (1980), *New World* (1986), *October* (1988) and *Democracy* (1991).

Themes
• The dream of "west"
• Restlessness and the desire for freedom
• Morality and the search for independence
• Mutual dependence
• Prostitution, violence and murder

Some other plays
Available from Playwrights Canada Press:
• *Cyrano de Bergerac*

Available from Red Deer Press:
• *Memoir*

Available from Talonbooks:
• *Democracy*
• *The Faraway Nearby*
• *Waiting for the Parade*

7 Stories

Morris Panych

Premiere: May 1989, *Arts Club Theatre*, Vancouver, British Columbia
Director: Morris Panych
Cast: 13 (6 women, 7 men); actors may play more than one part
Stage Setting: All action takes place on the 7th floor of an apartment building – on the ledge outside various windows
Publisher/Place/Year: Talonbooks, Vancouver, British Columbia 1990
Length: 101 pages
Performance Rights: Patricia Ney, Christopher Banks & Associates, 6 Adelaide St. E., Ste. 610, Toronto, Ontario M5C 1H6, 416-214-1155, fax 416-214-1150

Characters

MAN	JENNIFER
CHARLOTTE	LILLIAN
JOAN	RACHEL
NURSE WILSON	LEONARD
RODNEY	AL
MARSHALL	MICHAEL
PERCY	

Summary

A man, who remains unnamed throughout the play, is standing on the window ledge on the seventh floor of an apartment building preparing to launch himself into oblivion. But he is constantly distracted from his intention by other inhabitants of the seventh floor. During these interruptions, however, none of these neighbours seem to recognise the man's reason for being on the ledge. Instead of helping him they pester him with their own problems, ask him his opinion on various things and then finally disappear again into their own apartments. We meet, for instance, Rodney and Charlotte, a couple who seem to get their kicks out of almost killing each other; there is the psychiatrist, Leonard, who constantly misinterprets everything that is said to him and feels constantly under attack; and Marshall, who hides his real personality because he thinks his fiancée only really likes the *façade* that he projects and not the real "him" which she doesn't know at all.

During the course of the play it turns out that every one of the inhabitants of this block is crazier than the man himself who had wanted to commit suicide. At the end he is confronted with Lillian, a one-hundred-year-old woman who is in need of constant care, who advises him to jump if that's really what he wants. The jump does not have to be downwards, however, he should just let himself be carried away by the wind; then he would really be flying. The man actually does jump and flies with his umbrella to the ledge of another building. He lands there and then flies back. He wants to tell Lillian all about what has happened but she has passed away in the meantime. Thus he is left standing on the window ledge waiting for the next gust to carry him away.

Background and Commentary

Morris Panych grew up in Alberta and then moved to British Columbia where he went to study. He graduated in 1977 from the University of British Columbia. Later he went to an *avant-garde* theatre school in London and then worked for a while at the Grips Theater in Berlin. He has written many plays including *The Cost of Living* and *The Ends of the Earth*. *7 Stories* was the first of his plays that he directed himself.

Panych—or so he claims—was always interested in the philosophical questions pertaining to suicide ("Going forward also means leaving behind everything which we believe in"). *7 Stories* is the expression of his search for the meaning of life. The man on the ledge on the seventh floor is kept from committing suicide by the events and acts of despair at the other windows. He takes on the role of advisor and confidant and indeed becomes the one who answers all their needs although no one is aware of his needs, let alone waste any of their thoughts on him. While all the others are driven by fear and are fixated only on themselves, the man is the only one on the seventh floor who gets involved with the others.

The stories of the people in the other windows can be summed up as a whole, which reflects existential desperation, problematizes human relationships but which nevertheless provides an unexpected and joyous feeling of hope. *7 Stories* is comical, farcical and yet serious at the same time: a collection of parodying sketches which—each in its own way—illuminate the central question of the play.

Originally—it has been said—the action was going to take place in an elevator in which the central figure would be confronted by different people with different problems everywhere the elevator stopped. *7 Stories* is kept alive by a continuous flow of dialogues, each one following quickly on the heels of the other. In the Arts Club Theatre in Vancouver the piece was played without a break and lasted approximately one-and-a-half hours. Much was expected of the five actors who took on the job. Four of them were each required to play three different roles along with the actor who played the central role of "the man" throughout. The greatest demand put upon the actors was that they were constantly required to oscillate between the comical and the real. One particular aspect of the play is summed up by Ray Conlogue in his review of a 1991 production of the play: "This play is an example of that very rare and endangered species of theatre, the fable. It is also an example of that even rarer creature, the successful fable." (*The Globe & Mail*, 1st March 1991)

Canadian Broadcasting Corporation (CBC) in Vancouver summed up its praise for Panych's play in the following words: "Panych has mixed Magritte, Sartre, Woody Allen and the book *Hiob* with Buster Keaton and magical realism: a very special chemistry with a very special effect."

Themes
- Search for the meaning of life
- Normalcy and madness
- Anonymity and selfishness in the big city
- Suicide

Some other plays
Available from Harbour Publishing:
- *Last Call*

Available from Playwrights Canada Press:
- *The Story of A Sinking Man* (in *Singular Voices*)

Available from Talonbooks:
- *The Cost of Living*
- *The Ends of the Earth*
- *Girl in a Fish Bowl*
- *2B WUT UR*
- *Earshot*
- *Lawrence & Holloman*
- *Life Sentence & Other Stories*
- *Vigil*

Doc

Sharon Pollock

Premiere: April 1984
Director: Guy Sprung
Cast: 5 (3 women, 2 men)
Stage Setting: A house, props and furniture are kept to a minimum
Publisher/Place/Year: Playwrights Canada Press, Toronto, Ontario 1984;
    Broadview Press, Peterborough, Ontario, 2003
Length: 90 pages
Performance rights: Sharon Pollock through Playwrights Canada Press

Characters
Ev
Catherine
Katie
Bob
Oscar

Summary
    Doc is a complex family drama concerning the fates of Ev (Everett, a
doctor), his wife Bob (Eloise Roberts, a former nurse), their daughter
Catherine, who also appears as Katie (as a young girl), and Ev's lifelong
buddy Oscar.
    Doc is a chronologically non-linear play, so it cannot be so simply
described in terms of its plot. In basic terms it describes the inter-family

relationships of the three main characters, their development and the results thereof, with occasional interjections from Oscar.

Pollock clearly has an extremely clear idea of how the play is to be performed, as the opening scenes particularly are cluttered with almost dictatorial stage directions. There is little room for manoeuvre, but the directions are necessary due to the complexity of the plot development and action and also due to the time "shifts" which constantly occur.

Ev is a doctor who has put his career before everything, including his family, he has a close relationship with his assistant, Valma, but it is never made clear whether this is anything more than professional. He is tortured by the death of his mother, but throughout the play never finds the courage to open the letter she left on the night of her death, because he cannot bear the thought that she might have committed suicide. His wife Bob has worked her way up in the world from her poor background to become a nurse. But, married to Ev, her life loses direction and meaning. Unable to work as a nurse—Ev won't allow her to work in the same hospital as him—she finds herself unable to adapt to the role of housewife and mother. She descends into alcoholism, despair and self-disgust. Catherine and Katie are the same person, but not necessarily the same character. They share a history, but not all of it, and consequently frequently see things differently. As an adult Catherine retains her father's drive, but also her mother's fear of being caught in a rut. Oscar is also a doctor, but completely unlike Ev. He has grown up from being a lazy rich kid to being a lazy doctor. There is an implied affair between Oscar and Bob, as he is the only one who finds time for her. But apart from one kiss, this is something else that remains unresolved.

The story progresses in the form of jumps in time, Pollock's so-called "shifts." Sometimes these occur in rapid succession, sometimes they are further apart. Pollock makes no suggestions how these time shifts are to be realised, but one would assume clever use of spotlights would be necessary to focus the audience's attention on the characters in the action, while the others change appearance or swap positions in the dark.

Background and commentary

Sharon Pollock was born Mary Sharon Chalmers in 1936 in Fredericton, New Brunswick. She has written several plays with a socio-historic background. *Blood Relations* won the Governor General's Award for Drama in 1982. The author has been playwright-in-residence at both the National Arts Centre and Alberta Theatre Projects, as well as Artistic Director and Dramaturge at Theatre Calgary. She was head of the Banff Centre's Playwrights Colony for four years. Pollock lives in Calgary.

With *Doc* Pollock started on a project entirely different from her previous plays. The story of *Doc* involves her own history. She grew up as "the doctor's daughter." Her father was a highly ambitious physician and had, just like Ev in the play, a hospital named after him. And just like in the play the family felt neglected due to the father's devotion to his job. Pollock's mother died when Sharon was 16, and people said it was by her own hand. Again, as in the play, Pollock wanted to finally come to terms with this part of her own history. When the play was performed at the New Brunswick Theatre her father wrote a short note for the programme.

But *Doc* is not meant to be understood as an autobiographical play. It is rooted in Pollock's family background, but is close on being a stereotype, the stereotype of a family in which the father is a workaholic and his wife confined to the house, being equal but not treated as equal. Like Catherine in the play, Pollock came back to explore this man, who can neither be loved nor abhorred by the audience, loved for his devotion to his patients or abhorred for his treatment of the family.

When *Doc* was put on stage by Toronto Free Theatre in 1984, Amanda Pollock, the playwright's 16-year-old daughter, played Katie, the younger Catherine. The mirroring effect was taken to its utmost.

Most audiences may initially be confused by the scenes as they change between past and present all the time, but this confusion clears up quickly. The aforementioned production in 1984 used a chess board as floor, to emphasize how the characters are used by the father as figures but break out constantly. Darkened mirrors that gave the impression of shadows walking in the background only enhanced the feeling that the exorcism of the ghosts of the past is Pollock's main aim.

Themes
- Personal experiences with universal implications
- A father's devotion to his job and its impact on the family

Some other plays
Available from Playwrights Canada Press:
- *Sharon Pollock: Three Plays* (*Moving Pictures*, *Angel's Trumpet*, *End Dream*)
- *The Komagata Maru Incident* (in *Six Canadian Plays*)

Available from NeWest Press:
- *Blood Relations*
- *Generations*

Available from Red Deer:
- *Getting it Straight*

Available from Broadview Press:
- *Fair Liberty's Call*

Harlem Duet

Djanet Sears

Premiere: April 1997 *Tarragon Extraspace*; produced by *Nightwood Theatre*
Director: Djanet Sears
Cast: 3 women, 2 men, double bass and a cello
Stage Setting: Harlem at different periods of time (1928, 1860, the present), an apartment in a brownstone building; a tiny dressing room; on the steps to a blacksmith's forge
Publisher/Place/Year: Scirocco Drama, Winnipeg, Manitoba 1997
Length: 117 pages
Performance rights: Djanet Sears through Playwrights Canada Press

Characters
BILLIE/HER/SHE
OTHELLO/HIM/HE
MAGI
AMAH
MONA
CANADA
DOUBLE BASS
CELLO

Summary
   Harlem Duet is a love story, or perhaps three love stories, which take place at three different times in history. Or rather, looking at it from

another point of view, it is the story of three failed relationships. It autopsies the relationships to a certain extent without ever coming up with a definitive answer for their failure. But one thing remains the same. In every case the man leaves the woman for a white woman, a woman of a different race. In present-day Harlem, Billie is grieving the loss of Othello, who has left her to find his affections in the arms of a white woman, Mona. Thus *Harlem Duet* is a sort of prelude to Shakespeare's *Othello*, in that it provides a kind of prehistory to the love affair between Othello and Desdemona. In *Harlem Duet* it is Othello's first wife, Billie, who is the focus.

In the two parallel stories a similar plot is also developed. Him and Her are slaves and lovers in the year 1860. Her wants desperately to escape to liberty, to Canada, where Black people have been given their freedom. But Him is uncertain, he is secretly in love with the daughter of his white master. In a later scene we see the lamenting Her cradling the corpse of Him in her arms. He has a noose around his neck and it would appear he has been the victim of a lynching. In the Harlem of 1928 He and She are performers in a minstrel show. He longs for more; for the chance to play one of the great Shakespearian (white) roles and is also in love with a white woman, also called Mona. Before he has the chance to leave her he slits his throat with a razor.

It is, however, Billie's and Othello's relationship that is dissected in the greatest detail. For those in the audience who may have failed to notice the similarities in their fates, all the lovers are played by the same two actors. But the modern day versions are explored in much greater detail. With Billie and Othello the relationship is already over, even if the feelings are not gone. They are worlds apart. She is convinced that their problem is a race issue; that Othello has betrayed his people. He finds her arguments ridiculous and accuses her of a kind of inverted racism. He is the Martin Luther King to her Malcolm X. In her desperation she turns to ancient practices, such as Egyptian alchemy, to concoct a potion which will destroy him.

The one stabilizing factor is Billie's father, Canada. He is perhaps a metaphor for all the Blacks who left America to seek sanctuary in Canada – and that is indeed also his story. He comes back to make Billie see "sense" at the eleventh hour.

Yet there is no easy resolution in this play. Billie ends up on a mental ward: we never find out if Othello does indeed fall victim to her poison: even Canada himself isn't an ideal role model. But this is not the play's purpose; to provide answers. It serves much more as a means of raising issues and asking questions. The play is about love, but its major issue is race and how the Black community deals with and has had to deal with racism. This is also a vehicle for Black actors to explore these issues (the only white figure, Mona, appears only as an offstage character).

Background and commentary

When *Harlem Duet* premiered in 1997 it was an instant success with both the audience and the critics. In that year alone it won four Dora Mavor Moore Awards (for best play, best production, best director and best female performance) and the Chalmers Award. But the appreciation of the play came to its height when Sears was presented the Governor General's Award for Drama for it the following year.

Djanet Sears' father is from Guyana, her mother from Jamaica. They met as students in London, England, where Djanet was born. Together with her family she moved to Saskatoon when she was fifteen years old and from there to Toronto, where she has been living for many years.

But she started questioning her idea of home and belonging in 1984 on a tour through Africa. Travelling from one African country to another she became increasingly aware of the stereotyped, superficial and sometimes negative images of Black people portrayed on TV and elsewhere. After a trip to an oasis and the Tassili Plateau—the site of ten-thousand-year-old Saharan rock paintings—she replaced her English name Janet (meaning "near God") with the name of the oasis Djanet (meaning "Paradise"). She had found her African roots.

Harlem Duet is a manifestation of the struggle to find her identity – as a Black woman in the white society of Northern America. Based on Shakespeare's *Othello*, Sears ventured to write a prelude, a prequel to it, taking advantage of the fact that Othello in Shakespeare's play is already around fifty and does not seem to have had a life before the action of the play. With Billie, Sears inserts Othello into a Black community that he is striving to flee. Billie does not only find herself betrayed but also her race. "How does race enter the bedroom? How does race enter your relationship, when there are no white people around?" (Interview with A.-R. Glaap, 2001) the author is asking. What happens, if an integrationist and a separatist argue about love and relationships and try to avoid—or vice versa concentrate on—race as a determining element?

The play is set in modern communities as well as in the past. The apartment Billie and Othello share is situated on the crossing of Malcolm X and Martin Luther King boulevards and the constant fragments of speeches, important for the history of Black people in America, keep reminding us that not only a personal tragedy is being presented on stage. The premiere of *Harlem Duet* also coincided with the new-found idea of the "Othello Syndrome," invented by the press to describe the goings-on during the trial of O.J. Simpson.

But the play is set in three timelines: the 1860s before the abolition of slavery, 1928 during the so-called Harlem Renaissance and the present. The historic timelines end in Othello's death on stage by Billie's hand, but it is the time line of the present that sets out to explore Shakespeare's text. Alongside this it also explores Billie's ideas of race. Her American-ness is confused with her Jamaican roots and when her father turns up, her Canadian-ness is brought into consideration. "[It] evokes the time in which Canada provided refuge to escaped slaves from the United States; it also brings the Diaspora to Harlem" (Leslie Sanders: "Othello Deconstructed: Djanet Sears' *Harlem Duet*." In: Sears, Djanet: *Testifyin'. Contemporary African Canadian Drama.* Toronto: Playwrights Canada Press, 2000) thus linking the 1860s and the present plot, creating a continuum of Black people's history. When *Harlem Duet* was staged at Neptune's du Maurier Theatre in 2000, all three sets were permanently on stage just requiring the actors to change from one set to another, thus making this continuum visual.

One year before Shakespeare's play was first put on stage, Elizabeth I had banished all Blacks from England, so that Othello on stage was always seen as the epitome of an outsider, surreal as Blacks were not usually present in society. But in *Harlem Duet* the audience is forced to see the story from the Black point of view. Othello is not an outsider, an alien, he is a member of an all-Black community who is trying to get out.

In a way, it is Magi and Amah who bring a touch of "normalcy" into the play thus being something like commentators on stage, thus making the whole setting real and believable.

Are we to identify with any of the characters? "It's Billie's story, so we're more prone to identify with her. Or, if we can't identify, feel for her. But in a way, Othello has the argument, the intellectual argument, and Billie has the emotional one. [...] The play for me works best, when you agree with Billie and then think she's mad and agree with Othello. When he says: 'We're all the same in the end [...], anyway,' [...] he's not lying. So, when the play works best, it forces you to question your own ideas about race, because they are two imperfect characters who really form kind of a trapeze." (Djanet Sears, Interview with A.-R. Glaap, 2001)

Themes
- A revision of Shakespeare's *Othello* used to discuss issues about African culture in the Americas
- The intersection of race, gender and love
- A rhapsodic blues tragedy
- A play set in three timelines

Some other plays
Available from Playwrights Canada Press:
- *Harlem Duet* (in *Testifyin'*)

Available from Women's Press:
- *Afrika Solo*

Patience

Jason Sherman

Premiere: February 1998 *Tarragon Theatre*, Toronto, Ontario
Director: Ian Prinsloo
Cast: 6 men, 4 women
Stage Setting: at present, various locations in Toronto
Publisher/Place/Year: Playwrights Canada Press, Toronto, Ontario 1998
Length: 93 pages
Performance rights: Jeff Alpern, The Alpern Group, 15645 Royal Oak Road, Encino, CA 91436, 818-528-1111, jalpern@alperngroup.com

Characters
REUBEN
PETER
PAUL
MIKE
JANICE
THE RABBI
DONNA
FRANK
SARAH
LIZ

Summary

Patience is a furiously-paced play, told with a great deal of wit and charm. The action is almost filmic in its qualities and would pose a great challenge for any stage director. Although a great deal of the plot is linear it is interspersed with flashbacks, which sometimes follow each other in such rapid succession that it is a huge test of any director's calibre to set them in scene in a way that the audience realise what is going on.

The play tells the story of Reuben, a businessman and family man, who is standing on the brink of the greatest deal in his company's history. The "Korean" deal will make him a very rich man. One evening he has a chance meeting with Paul in a Chinese restaurant. Paul sits down to join him and to tell him how he has sold his company, and how giving up the stable life he enjoyed enabled him to finally realize his dream, a dream that he has suppressed for many years for the sake of a quiet life. He says he is going to Vancouver to make a film about a man who has everything and then suddenly loses it all. And after wallowing for a while in self-pity, the man realises that he has lost these things because he never should have had them in the first place – this finally gives him the freedom to find his true self.

Reuben is dubious, but right after this meeting things start going wrong for him. When he comes home he finds his furious wife clutching a handful of love letters. She throws him out of the house, unwilling to even hear that the letters are ten years old and that he is happier now with her than he has ever been. The betrayal is enough to destroy his marriage. Reuben is confused and hurt and meets up with his friend Mike who tells him that the very Paul, with whom he was sitting in a restaurant the previous night, had in fact died on the way to Vancouver a year previously. Reuben calls Sarah, Paul's wife and the woman with whom he had exchanged those love letters ten years before, and she confirms her husband's death.

Then another phone call summons Reuben to his office, where he is told by his partners that they are throwing him out of the company, that he, in fact, is the one factor holding them all back. Reuben is devastated. His life and the future he had dreamed of really have been taken from him, like the man in Paul's story.

As Reuben renews his friendship with Sarah, Paul's wife, the flashbacks tell the story of what has gone on before. Reuben also makes contact with his brother Phil and his girlfriend Liz. The audience sees the events that have led to Reuben's emotional crisis, and also that it is something not solved so lightly. As Reuben's relationship with Sarah develops into something more than a friendship, it becomes clear that Liz's feelings for him are not completely platonic. A chance meeting with a rabbi brings Reuben's "Jewishness" back to the surface, but serves more as a vehicle to demonstrate that it is something he has, to a great extent, left behind him.

Patience is also a play where the issues are not resolved, rather they are highlighted. And it is clear that Reuben himself has not yet fully worked out the issues of his past. Yet he has learned enough to reject Liz's advances even though he is just as attracted to her as she is to him. In the last few scenes, the flashbacks become ever quicker and the action becomes more and more hectic. Thoughts and feelings are mixed up. The action is no longer linear, yet retains its own logic. There is a bigger picture that is presented here, but the audience is left to draw its own conclusions.

Background and commentary

As one reviewer put it, *Patience* is a "dark, complex morality play packed with jokes," (Kate Taylor, *The Globe and Mail*, 6th March 1998) and its subject is no less than the meaning of life itself. Indeed, the audience gets the impression that this is a black comedy with underlying streams of bleak philosophy when seeing Reuben—who has so far been neglectful of his family, business partner and morals—lose everything, all the cornerstones that define his life, within a matter of hours.

Whenever a control freak loses control and starts exploring "the meaning of it all" the character is irredeemably changed, but whether Reuben changes at all is left open by Sherman; it is Paul who in the end soliloquizes about the meaninglessness of life.

Jason Sherman was born in 1962 in Montreal and has lived in Toronto since 1969. He is author of several plays that have been highly acclaimed and won him several awards (The Governor General's Literary Award for Drama for *Three in the Back, Two in the Head* in 1995 and the Chalmers Award for *The League of Nathans* in 1993).

Patience has been criticized for the jokes Sherman makes at the expense of his religion. And it has been said that the interlude with the rabbi in Act Two seems superfluous, his farcical conversation with Yahweh on the mobile phone too ludicrous for the concept as such.

But, nevertheless, the play is a powerful exploration of a person who deemed himself in control of his life and other people, and all of a sudden cannot but realize how weak the basis of such power is. He finds himself dropped by people he thought he was controlling.

Interestingly, the power the play exerts on the audience stems from a pessimism that does not drag you down but sets your mind going.

Themes
- The meaning of life
- Existential loneliness
- A world of personal happiness turning to dust
- The biblical story of Job as a foil

Some other plays
Available from Playwrights Canada Press:
- *An Acre of Time*
- *It's All True*
- *Jason Sherman: Six Plays* (excludes *An Acre of Time*)
- *Reading Hebron*
- *League of Nathans*
- *The Retreat*
- *Three in the Back, Two in the Head*

The Saints
and Apostles

Raymond
Storey

Premiere: 17ᵗʰ April 1990, *Theatre Passe Muraille* as part of the Buddies in Bad Times' *4-Play Festival*
Director: Edward Roy
Cast: 5 (2 women, 3 men)
Stage Setting: Various settings including: empty room with three shrines, a balcony, a bistro
Publisher/Place/Year: Playwrights Canada Press, Toronto, Ontario 1991
Length: 90 pages
Performance rights: Raymond Storey storeyinc@earthlink.net

Characters
MICHAEL
MADELINE
DANIEL
PETER
RITA

Summary
Daniel has newly arrived in Toronto and looks up Michael, a fleeting acquaintance from before. At first Michael is less than enthusiastic, but then falls head over heels in love with Daniel. This leaves him feeling very confused because up to this point he had led a very sober life where there was no place for deep emotions.

After a while Daniel, who is HIV positive and thus is daily confronted with the prospect of death, draws himself away from Michael and
returns to live with his father because he doesn't want to force himself into
anyone's life and, above all, does not want to give rise to the tearful end of
a relationship. His personal drama is his reality and so he has little understanding for the sentimentality of the healthy. At the end of the play he
turns up again and delivers a monologue: he has, however, no more contact to the other characters. What he wants is to face his coming death
alone and for Michael to try to put his own life, which has been so fleet-
ingly yet intensely touched by Daniel, in order without him.

Parallel to the main plotline the audience sees excerpts from
Michael's relationship with his mother, Rita, and his housemate Madeline.
Both relationships are affected by the changes in Michael's relationship
with Daniel. Because of this Michael allows his mother, for the first time
in years, back into his life, he also starts taking more notice of Maddie. For
a long time he has taken her for granted but now he finally realises how
important she really is to him.

Background and Commentary

Millennium Approaches and *Perestroika*, two plays by the American
author Tony Kushner, which were successfully performed in many
European countries under the umbrella title *Angels in America,* can really
lay claim to significantly raising the level of awareness about the plague of
our times, AIDS. The Canadian play *The Saints and the Apostles* is also a
play about AIDS. But in this play the author is not exclusively concerned
with the people who suffer from the disease, but rather those with and
around them who are also affected. Whereas those who suffer from AIDS
are reliant on understanding and even love, those around them often draw
themselves back and remain silent. They do not want to know about people who do not have long left on this earth. Storey is unable to solve this
problem and doesn't even try to. In a public statement released by
Workshop West Theatre in Edmonton in 1991 he said: "It is with regret
that I found out how limited my own ability to change the world is. I am
just someone who tells the stories. The only thing that I can do is to make
sure I tell the story as honestly and convincingly as possible – on subjects
like these: the fear of intimacy; the desperate longing for love; the search
for dignity; the necessity of having hope."

It is Storey's belief that only those who do not suffer from the disease
are in a position to learn. Those suffering from AIDS are the "saints" in
this piece; they lose everything which was important to them in their rela-
tionship(s). The people who survive them limit themselves to looking for
blame, to mutual admonishment and to observe moral standards at all
costs. They talk of "them" and "us." Storey first felt the need to write about
AIDS when he returned to his home town of Toronto in 1989 and found

that several of his friends and acquaintances had shortly before died of AIDS, a disease which at the time was not so well known and had been dismissed as "yet another American problem." The play was originally written as a solo piece for a benefit concert for a hospice for AIDS sufferers; it was soon developed into a full-blown play with five characters who reflect the attitudes of people in our times towards AIDS: making AIDS a taboo subject and prejudices can develop all too easily into indifference and disinterest. But the play refuses to let itself be too easily categorised and that is, in the words of Liz Nicholls, "what makes the play so appealing [...] that it snubs the categories – like gay love story, or chin-up AIDS 'comedy' or even hip gay/straight odd couple roommate sit-com." (*The Edmonton Journal*, 10th November 1991)

"What would you do?" asks Storey. "How would you redefine your priorities, if the first person you've ever really loved suddenly becomes the most dangerous person in your life?"

Raymond Storey is also well known for a book about the sour-gas industry, *Something in the Wind,* which he wrote in 1984.

Themes
- Living with AIDS
- HIV positive people and those around them
- Taboos and prejudices
- Confrontation of death
- Conflict between generations

Some other plays
Available from Playwrights Canada Press:
- *Angel of Death*

Available from Playwrights Guild of Canada:
- *Country Chorale*
- *The Dreamland*
- *The Girls in the Gang*
- *The Last Bus*

Available from Scirocco:
- *The Glorious 12th*

Someday

Drew Hayden Taylor

Premiere: 4th November 1991, *De-ba-jeh-mu-jig Theatre* at Wikwemikong Reserve, Ontario
Directors: Larry Lewis/Floyd Favel
Cast: 4 (3 women, 1 man)
Stage setting: A fictional Ojibway community on the Otter Lake Reserve, central Ontario
Publisher/Place/Year: Fifth House Publishers, Saskatoon, Saskatchewan 1993
Length: 81 pages
Performance rights: Aurora Artists, Janine Cheeseman, 19 Wroxeter Avenue, Toronto, Ontario M4K 1J5, 416-463-4634, fax 416-463-4889

Characters
RODNEY: 25 years old; friend of the family
BARB WABUNG: 23 years old; Rodney's girlfriend
ANNE WABUNG: 53 years old; Barb's and Janice's mother
JANICE (GRACE) WIRTH: 35 years old; long lost daughter/sister

Summary

The week before Christmas 1991 in a fictional Ojibway community in central Ontario. The preparations are in full swing when Anne Wabung suddenly makes the happy discovery when reading the newspaper, that she has won five million dollars in the lottery.

A short time later she gets a call from her long lost elder daughter Grace who was taken from her at the age of seven months by the white Children's Aid. Grace's father had been working at the time in the army – a fact that no one was allowed to find out. The Children's Aid assumed that the father had run out on the family and took Anne's baby away. She said nothing because she had promised her husband that she would tell nobody where he was.

Grace speaks to Rodney on the telephone and tells him that she will visit the next day, Christmas day. Anne is overjoyed, tidies up the whole house, cooks food and generally makes everything ready for Grace's visit. Barb, on the other hand, is skeptical and a little jealous: now of all times, when Anne has just become suddenly rich, the long lost sister calls up out of the blue – after thirty-five years of silence! Moreover she feels a little forgotten by her mother, who is so involved with her preparations for the visit.

Everyone, however, is quite excited as Grace finally arrives. She turns out to be pretty, successful and well-groomed, and is rather embarrassed as the dye from her now wet Italian designer shoes runs. Trying to cover her embarrassment she just makes things worse as she first stains Rodney's shirt and then knocks over a chair. She then proceeds in her ignorance to ask several inappropriate questions. While flicking through the family photo album she asks who the young man is in one of the pictures. Anne is very upset, because it is the son she lost in a road accident some years before. Grace seeks to find out by questioning Anne and Barb what the real reasons were that she was taken into care. That the actual reason was the unexplained whereabouts of her father, Grace, or Janice as she is now known, finds it a bit hard to swallow. She feels somewhat betrayed and wants to leave immediately: she feels she no longer belongs here. No one can persuade her to stay. When they ask her when she will come back she replies with a vague "Oh someday, I suppose," and climbs into her car and drives away.

Background and commentary

Among Native playwrights one in particular has made a name for himself in the early nineties. A young dramatist born in the Curve Lake reservation in Ontario in 1962: Drew Hayden Taylor. He is an Ojibway who lived initially with his mother and her family on the reservation, later going to college in Toronto where he has now lived for some years.

Indigenous dramatists get their feelings off their chests about the maltreatment of Natives in the past in different ways. Taylor has no program; he orients himself on reality, his own reality. He talks about experiences that he has had, or his mother, or his family and clarifies these experiences in terms of individual people. *Someday* (1992) deals with the so-called scoop-up operation of the sixties, a government program that planned to take Native children and give them up for adoption. The name of this program in Saskatchewan was AIM – *Adopt Indian Métis*. In 1990 Taylor wrote a short story for *The Globe and Mail* newspaper which he was then commissioned to rework into a play. The central idea of the scoop-up was that Native children, through their adoption by whites, would be taken out of their own culture and would become part of Canadian (white) culture. This sort of adoption was a relatively new idea in the Canada of the nineteen-sixties.

Someday reflects something that happened in many of Canada's provinces. The piece brings to the surface the frustration still felt today by many Natives, who had felt like second class citizens at the time. It was not until 1960 that Natives were given the vote. Nowadays Natives can raise their voices and articulate their feelings and opinions. One of the main reasons that Drew Hayden Taylor wrote *Someday* was to make the feelings of Native people, their bitterness and also their anger both visible and audible. He wants to bring home to audiences what has happened to Native peoples during the last two hundred years, how Natives have been forced to accept considerable losses to their culture and languages. One prediction pessimistically anticipates that only three out of twenty-three aboriginal languages will survive the next twenty-five years: Ojibway, Cree and Inuit. Taylor himself hardly speaks Ojibway any more; he and the majority of Native playwrights write in English. In one distinct way, however, Taylor is different from the others: he wants to show that Natives—regardless of their cultural and linguistic differences—are no different to any other people anywhere else. "These are Natives, they act and react the way they do. Can you [a non-Native] see yourself in here?" said the author in an interview. He believes that people in many different countries have a rather romantic idea about Indians and Inuit [Eskimos]. This, in his opinion, is just a short step away from racism.

One thing, however, is of particular importance to Taylor: he considers himself to be a Native who doesn't write about culture-specific aspects, peculiarities and events but rather about those aspects of culture which bridge the gaps between Natives and non-Natives. For this reason he is a very significant representative of the young generation of Native writers in Canada.

One particular piece from this author which is especially well-suited for youth theatre audiences or TYA is *Toronto at Dreamers Rock*, a dramatised "coming of age" story. It is the story of a sixteen-year-old Ojibway who learns from two other Ojibway boys (one from 400 years in the past and one from 100 years in the future) at Dreamer's Rock that he is an important linking element between the past and all its traditions and the demands of the technological future.

Themes
• Legal position of Canadian Indians
• Dream and reality
• The effects of political decisions on the individual
• Romantic preconceptions about Natives
• Natives and non-Natives: specifics and common characteristics

Some other plays
Available from Fifth House:
• *Bootlegger Blues*
• *Education is Our Right*
• *Toronto at Dreamer's Rock*

Available from Talonbooks:
• *alter-Natives*
• *The Boy in the Treehouse*
• *Girl Who Loved Her Horses*

Lion in the Streets

Judith Thompson

Premiere: June 1990, as part of the *duMaurier World Stage Theatre Festival*, Toronto, Ontario; *duMaurier Theatre Centre*

Director: Judith Thompson

Cast: 27 (16 women, 11 men); original production featured 6 actors (4 women, 2 men) playing multiple roles.

Stage Setting: Various settings: a playground, a park, an apartment, a church

Publisher/Place/Year: Coach House Press, Toronto, Ontario 1992; Playwrights Canada Press, Toronto, Ontario 1996

Length: 53 pages

Performance rights: Shain Jaffe, Great North Artists, 350 Dupont Street, Toronto, Ontario M5R 1V9, 416-925-2051, fax 416-925-3904

Characters

ISOBEL

NELLIE, LAURA, ELAINE, CHRISTINE, SHERRY

RACHEL, LILY, RHONDA, ELLEN, SCARLETT

SCALATO, TIMMY, GEORGE, DAVID, RODNEY, BEN

MARTIN, ISOBEL'S FATHER, RON, FATHER HAYES, MICHAEL

SUE, JILL, JOANNE, BECCA, JOAN

Summary

Lion in the Streets is not a drama in the conventional sense; it is more a series of different scenes which are all connected by the presence of a murdered nine-year-old Portuguese girl, Isobel, and where one character from the previous scene becomes the protagonist in the next scene.

The piece presents the problems and crises that are omnipresent in big-city life. The audience finds out that Bill cheats on his wife Sue with Lily, and that Sue confronts him in her desperation and humiliates herself; that the parents' committee argues about the value or danger of using sweets as rewards for children; that Joanne is dying of bone cancer and wants to commit suicide and wants Rhonda to help her and so on.

Now and then the audience ask themselves whether and to what extent what they see is reality. Because no sooner have they seen Rodney cutting Michael's, his lover's, throat in a passionate row, then the audience hears Sherry, Rodney's colleague, telling her boyfriend that Rodney has been in the office all day shouting at some imaginary person. Did Rodney really commit murder or not?

At the beginning of the play Isobel does not know who it is who killed her seventeen years ago. She only finds out gradually as she slips from one scene to another and listens to the various conversations of the other characters. While she is searching, at the beginning, for someone who will take her home, at the end she is looking for someone to take her to heaven. Sherry, who is forced to tell her pathologically jealous boyfriend about her rape down to the smallest detail just because he wants to hear her speaking, breaks down under this psychological pressure and takes Isobel to the cemetery where she sees her murderer Ben. Instead of taking revenge on him she forgives him and asks the audience at the end of the play—now as an adult—to take control of their own lives. Lost in her thoughts she then climbs up to heaven.

Background and Commentary

Along with Brad Fraser, Judith Thompson has decisively shaped the contours of Canadian drama in the eighties and nineties and also helped make Canadian drama known outside of Canada. Fraser's *Unidentified Human Remains and the True Nature of Love* and Thompson's *Lion in the Streets* were, for example, both very successfully performed at the Hampstead Theatre in London in the spring of 1993. The well-known critic Benedict Nightingale began his review of the London production of *Lion in the Streets* with the words: "Whoever still thinks of Canada as a wooded wilderness at the end of the world which is only worth mentioning because of its mounted police, its lumberjacks, mountains and maple trees doesn't know much about the theatre exports of this country."

Both Fraser and Thompson are unimpressed by the tradition of the "well made play"; both deal with the problems of identity crises in the chaos of the big city. Thompson's Toronto is a city full of glittering colours but an all the more threatening and dangerous place. It is not the Toronto of the profit-seekers on Bay Street or Yonge Street, rather that of her own neighbourhood. Her plays are about dissatisfaction with modern civilisation. The lion of the title is not at all the "King of the beasts;" it is a hungry lion in a silver automobile and represents the wild beasts who are looking for an outlet from the daily grind. Its snarl means threatening and lethal danger. The people show signs of deep inner insecurity and their vain attempts to win back their lost innocence.

The ghost of the murdered Portuguese girl who wanders the Toronto streets is confronted by a series of very different people – mostly suspicious-looking and down-and-out people. And then when she finally finds her murderer she cries to us, the audience, and begs us to make use of our lives and not to waste them.

In an interview in 1995 Judith Thompson answered the question as to what she considers her contribution to contemporary Canadian drama to be, in the following way: "I believe that it is something unconscious in my character that I want to make visible. My plays are first and foremost psychological journeys of discovery. They try to recognise where the conscious and the unconscious meet, how they work together, how they collide and cause conflicts."

Thompson wants to shed light on the human psyche, which remains mostly hidden, which is an explanation, in her opinion, why people so often react so violently: "People want to live behind closed doors. They don't want the doors to be opened so that light can shine in."

Lion in the Streets is, as already mentioned, not a play in the conventional sense. The individual scenes are only linked by the ghost of the nine-year-old Isobel who wanders through the streets. In this way the audience is taken on a journey through the lives of nearly thirty characters, played by five actors in eleven scenes. The only figure who is constantly present is that of Isobel who gets caught up in the lives of these people and wants to find out where she really is. Many of the characters are never heard or met by the other characters, just by the audience. They reflect the inability some people have to express themselves. And if the construction principles of *Lion in the Streets* don't seem immediately clear to the audience then there is a good reason for this. It is a reflection of the experiences of the people that are being described.

Lion in the Streets is a play without a real plot, rather it is densely packed with impressions; a series of razor-sharp vignettes which constitute a mosaic, a mosaic of everyday people who live in the big city jungle as though they were caught in a trap from which there is no escaping. A modern Inferno. Ray Conlogue, in *The Globe and Mail*, describes it as a "daisy chain play." He goes on to explain:

Each scene is a mini-drama, apparently standing alone. But it always contains [at least] one character from the previous mini-drama. [...] This is how people really live in cities: Not in a self-contained community, but connected by tendrils to a series of different worlds. (*The Globe and Mail*, 8th November 1990)

When Isobel's ghost finally finds the man who had murdered her seventeen years earlier, she picks up a stick and is on the verge of killing him. But then, at the last moment, she lets the stick fall to the ground and says to him: "I love you." In the above quoted interview with Judith Thompson, I asked her what had inspired her to write such an ending and whether she herself would have killed the murderer: "I wrote it spontaneously and I don't think I would've killed him." After contemplating this for a while, she then added: "I don't think much of the death penalty because I don't agree with continuing the cycle of violence [...] forgiveness not revenge is what we need."

Lion in the Streets continues the series of plays that has made Judith Thompson into one of the best known and most admired Canadian playwrights: *The Crackwalker* (1980), *White Biting Dog* (1984), *I Am Yours* (1987).

The author herself was born in Montréal in 1954, studied at Queens University and at the National Theatre School. She was active as an actor at the Manitoba Theatre Centre and Toronto Arts Productions. The immediate success of *The Crackwalker* allowed her to dedicate her life exclusively to playwrighting. She is also the recipient of two Governor General's Literary Awards for Drama. She lives together with her husband and five children in the Annex Area of Toronto.

In the interview, Judith Thompson was also asked if there was anything specifically Canadian in her plays. She answered: "My plays come from my surroundings in Toronto. But they are also somehow *un-Canadian* because they are not at all friendly and reserved; they don't put up with anything and in that way they reveal Canada's alter ego."

Themes
• Self-discovery and self-acceptance
• Murder and rape
• The modern city as a place of threat and danger
• Incapability of socialising in the modern class society

Some other plays
Available from Playwrights Canada Press:
• *The Crackwalker*   • *Sled*
• *I Am Yours*   • *Perfect Pie*
• *Habitat*   • *White Biting Dog*
• *Judith Thompson – 20th Century Plays 1980-2000* (includes *Pink* plus all of the above except *Habitat*)

Albertine, in Five Times/ Albertine, en cinq temps

Michel Tremblay

Premiere (Fr.): 12ᵗʰ October 1984, *Théâtre Français du Centre National des Arts,* Ottawa, Ontario
Director: André Brassard
Premiere (Eng.): 9ᵗʰ April 1985, *Tarragon Theatre,* Toronto, Ontario
Director: Bill Glassco
Cast: 6 women (Albertine at the ages of 30, 40, 50, 60, 70 and one other woman)
Stage Setting: Various locations including a restaurant and an old people's home
Publisher/Place/Year: (Fr.) Leméac, Ottawa, Ontario 1984; (Eng.) Talonbooks, Vancouver, British Columbia 1986
Running time: 1 hour 30
Performance rights: J. C. Goodwin et Associates, 839 est, rue Sherbrooke, Suite 2, Montréal, Québec H2L 1K6, 514-598-5252, fax 514-598-1878

Characters
ALBERTINE: at the ages of 30, 40, 50, 60, and 70
MADELEINE

Summary

The seventy-year-old Albertine moves into an old people's home and reflects on her catastrophic life. Her son has completely withdrawn into himself and lives in a home for disturbed people; her daughter committed suicide in the seventies. She herself has never been able to cultivate a close relationship with anyone apart from her sister Madeleine – not even with her own husband. While she thinks about her life she talks to her other selves who tell snatches of the story each from her own temporal perspective. The Albertines from different periods attack each other constantly. The older ones tell the younger ones what they ought to do: the younger ones criticise the older ones for having forgotten what used to be important to them. However, in all of these sometimes very aggressive discussions one sees the desire to really understand at least oneself, if not the rest of the world.

Background and Commentary

Born in 1942, Michel Tremblay came under the influence of the cultural movement which was brought about by the so-called Quiet Revolution in Québec and which found its expression in the theatre of psychological realism, the willingness to experiment and in direct political statements. Critics consider the successful synthesis of these three elements in Tremblay's works to be particularly praiseworthy. Tremblay first made his name with the play *Les Belles-Sœurs* (1968). The French language literary magazine *Lire* claimed in 1987 in an article with the title "The ideal theatre library" that *Les Belles-Sœurs* was one of forty-nine plays which were essential for anyone interested in the development of theatre. Since then Tremblay has become one of the best known Québécois playwrights. He has written some twenty plays and several film scripts. His works have been acknowledged world-wide; they have been translated into more than twenty different languages. Since the early nineties he has become extremely popular in Scotland; *Hosanna, La Maison Suspendue* and *Forever Yours, Marie-Lou* have all been translated into Scottish. Tremblay himself recommended *Albertine, in Five Times*, original title *Albertine, en cinq temps,* for inclusion in this book. The first performance of the English version of the play, translated by Bill Glassco and John van Burek, took place in 1986 in the Tarragon Theatre in Toronto. Albertine, who comes from a working class neighbourhood in Montréal, looks back at some of the most important moments of her life which are all characterised by failure and disappointment. Five actresses take over the roles of Albertine, one for each of the decades of her life represented, as a 30-, 40-, 50-, 60- and 70-year-old. The five Albertines are all on stage at the same time, sometimes not noticing one another, sometimes talking with each other, sometimes haggling. Alongside them appears Albertine's sister Madeleine whose life has run quite differently to Albertine's and whose age is not revealed. She fills a role as a sort of "chorus" to the dialogues which Albertine conducts with her various selves.

The seventy-year-old Albertine has undergone such a personality change that she is now hardly to be compared with her younger selves. She has hardly achieved anything noteworthy in her life but at the end the outstanding features of her character are goodness and dignity.

Albertine, en cinq temps is far more than a parable about the enslavement of Québec by the economic "heavyweights" of English-speaking Canada, as some theatre critics in the mid-eighties thought. *Albertine, en cinq temps* is one of those Canadian plays which, starting from specifically Canadian themes, arrives at the universal, and for this reason is also of great interest to audiences outside of Canada. The Canadian context is the area of Montréal, the working-class area, in which the author grew up. The play is typical of the liberal social criticism that one finds in most of Tremblay's work: "What I am criticising in our society is that it is based on competition between men." He makes an effort to let women have their say, women wherever and whenever. The specific structure of society in Quebec is just a peg to hang it on. It is about everything that people have in common – their worries, their suffering, their dreams, their yearnings. Knowledge about these things paves the way for better mutual understanding. Albertine would not be so convincing if the play were merely a portrait of working-class women in Montreal.

The performance of *Albertine, en cinq temps* is challenging for both actors and director. Sensibility and fury are the two poles between which the action swings. Because the five women who represent the different phases of Albertine's life appear simultaneously—rather than one after the other—on the stage, a great degree of concentration is required on the individual experiences as well as the connecting link that holds them all together. None of the actresses plays a complete character. Together they express the various changing and contradictory facets which make up Albertine's churned up personality.

The performance of the play lasts about one-and-a-half hours without a break. As Pat Donnelly, in *The Gazette*, jocularly remarked: "Eugene O'Neill invented the five-hour play in order to bring the perspective of a lifetime to an evening in the theatre. Fortunately, Tremblay gets to the point a bit sooner than that." (*The Gazette*, Montréal, 23rd May 1985) At the end one meets an Albertine who is—as one Canadian actress who played her said—a wonderful woman who could have been one of the greats if she had lived in different circumstances.

Themes
- Consideration of one's own values and behaviour patterns
- Breaking away from one's own past
- The problem of ageing
- Women in a "man's" world
- From Canadian context to universal statements

Some other plays
- *Les Belles-Sœurs* (Leméac Éditeur)
  Les Belles-Sœurs – English translation by Bill Glassco and John Van Burek (Talonbooks)
- *Bonjour, là Bonjour* (Leméac Éditeur)
  Bonjour, là Bonjour – English translation by Bill Glassco (Talonbooks)
- *La Duchese de Langeais* (Leméac Éditeur)
  La Duchese de Langeais – English translation by John Van Burek (Talonbooks)
- *A toi, pour toujours, ta Marie-Lou* (Leméac Éditeur)
  Forever Yours Marie-Lou – English translation by John Van Burek (Talonbooks)
- *Hosanna* (Leméac Éditeur)
  Hosanna – English translation by Bill Glassco and John Van Burek (Talonbooks)
- *La Maison Suspendue* (Leméac Éditeur)
- *St. Carmen of the Main* – English translation by John Van Burek (Talonbooks)
- *La Vrai Monde?* (Leméac Éditeur)
  The Real World? – English translation by Bill Glassco and John Van Burek (Talonbooks)
- *Encore une fois, si vous permettez* (Leméac Éditeur)
  For the Pleasure of Seeing Her Again – English translation by Linda Gaboriau (Talonbooks)
- *Twelve Opening Acts*
- *Impromptu On Nun's Island*

Fronteras Americanas

Guillermo Verdecchia

Premiere: January 1993, *Tarragon Theatre Extraspace*, Toronto, Ontario
Director: Jim Warren
Cast: 1 man (in different costumes)
Stage Setting: Empty stage
Publisher/Place/Year: Coach House Press, Toronto, Ontario 1993; Talonbooks, Vancouver, British Columbia 1997
Length: 64 pages
Performance rights: Angela Wright, Noble Talent Management, 2411 Yonge Street, Suite 202, Toronto, Ontario M4P 2E7 416-482-6556

Characters
VERDECCHIA
WIDELOAD

Summary
For many years Verdecchia has wanted to visit Argentina, the country he left as a youth, but the fear of being conscripted into the army has stopped him thus far. After Pinochet's fall he finally decides to go. On his first day there, someone is shot outside his hotel room. He feels like a stranger in his own land, where he is regarded as a tourist, but equally so in his adopted country, Canada, where he is considered a foreigner. While Verdecchia attempts to find his own identity in his fragmentary memories, he is continually interrupted by Wideload who ridicules the reservations

that North Americans (and also Europeans) have about anyone who is not the same as them. He is the archetypal naive and child-like Latino who doesn't let the audience realise until much later that it is they who are being laughed at and not the other way round. The history of North and South America is brought just as much into play as the Iran-Contra affair, the Free Trade Agreement and other popular media clichés.

At the end of the play Verdecchia appeals to the audience to free themselves from spatially defined classification of identity and to live "on the border," to remember their history, their predecessors and different identities and to build themselves a new, more rounded personality from their knowledge of all these things.

Background and Commentary

Guillermo Verdecchia, the author of *Fronteras Americanas,* is an actor and dramatist. He was born in Argentina and lives in Canada. He came to prominence with his 1991 play *The Noam Chomsky Lectures*, which he produced together with Daniel Brooks. For *Fronteras Americanas* [American Borders] he was awarded the Governor General's Literary Award for Drama in 1993. He wrote the play after visiting the country of his birth. The play is an intelligent as well as funny satire on stereotypes and clichés which frequently disturb if not destroy relations between different cultures. It is about prejudices against people from Latin America who are not infrequently labelled as bullfighters, mad dictators, guileless farmers, tango dancers or players of guitar music.

The actor in this play attempts to find his own niche between two cultures, to live on the borders and to break down stereotypes. Because he slips into a second role with increasing frequency throughout the play, the play develops more and more into a dialogue between the two characters. One of them tells of his experiences as a tourist in his own country, Argentina, but also as a citizen of Canada, where he still feels like a foreigner. He is looking for his own identity by means of his own memories. The other comments derisively on the stereotypical prejudices Americans have about everything that is strange to them. The audience is left increasingly with the impression that the man who presents himself as a satirist is himself part of the satire. Film clips and slides which are projected onto a screen onstage, portraits of Christopher Columbus and Rita Moreno, as well as quotes from Bolivar, Fuentes and Paz and Speedy Gonzalez caricatures all serve to add weight to the sideswipes and comments.

Fronteras Americanas is a sturdy basis for the clarification of the problem of discrimination in a multicultural society. The piece can be produced with minimal costs and is particularly good for small theatres.

Themes
- Canada as a multicultural society
- Canada as a part of the American continent
- Meaning of nationality for identity
- The hidden discrimination in prejudices and clichés

Some other plays
Available from Playwrights Guild of Canada:
- *Final Decisions/War*

Available from Playwrights Canada Press:
- *Freedom Fighters* (in *Instant Applause*)

Available from Talonbooks:
- *Line in the Sand*
- *Noam Chomsky Lectures*

Zastrozzi – The Master of Discipline

George F. Walker

Premiere: November 1977, *Toronto Free Theatre*, Toronto, Ontario
Director: William Lane
Cast: 6 (2 women, 4 men)
Stage Setting: The ruins of an ancient city in Europe (probably Italy) in the 1890's
Publisher/Place/Year: Playwrights Canada Press, Toronto, Ontario 1979; In: *Modern Canadian Drama*, Talonbooks, Vancouver, British Columbia
Length: 86 pages
Performance rights: Shain Jaffe, Great North Artists, 350 Dupont Street, Toronto, Ontario M5R 1V9, 416-925-2051, fax 416-925-3904

Characters
ZASTROZZI: a master criminal; a German
BERNARDO: his friend
VEREZZI: an artist, dreamer; an Italian
VICTOR: his tutor
MATILDA: a gypsy; a raven-haired beauty
JULIA: an aristocrat; a fair-haired beauty

Summary
Italy in the 19th century. Many years ago Verezzi has murdered Zastrozzi's mother but has no memory of the event. Zastrozzi has been hunting the *artiste* for three years in order to wreak his revenge. Verezzi,

however, who considers himself to be a saint and is becoming ever more eccentric, has managed to elude him because he has been helped by Victor, an ex-priest, who is bound to him by an old promise. One day, however, Zastrozzi confronts Verezzi. Initially he decides by means of a devious plan to drive his adversary to commit suicide. When this does not succeed he takes up his sword and makes his way to an old jail where Verezzi has hidden himself in the meantime. More or less coincidentally all of the other characters meet each other there. In a somewhat comical showdown, Julia kills Matilda, Bernardo kills Julia, Zastrozzi kills Bernardo and then finally Victor. Only Verezzi, who has slept through all this in a corner, survives the bloodshed. Zastrozzi wakes him but doesn't kill him because it suddenly occurs to him that he is no longer filled with the need to hunt Verezzi down. But he still needs a purpose. He sends Verezzi away giving him a day's head start in order that he can start the hunt over again.

Background and Commentary

George F. Walker's play is the oldest of the plays to be introduced in this book. It was written in 1977 and was based on a novelette of the same name—written by ten-year-old Percy Bysshe Shelley—in which Europe's greatest criminal, Zastrozzi, tirelessly hunts Verezzi, not only because he has taken part in the murder of Zastrozzi's mother but also because Zastrozzi doesn't like his smile. Superficially the play seems to be a melodrama but it should also be seen as a morality play. The central theme is evil and the central question is: who, in a godless world, can punish evil and judge evildoers. Zastrozzi is the incarnation of evil. He is out for revenge although at the last he is somewhat vague about the real reasons for it. His thinking and his striving is all directed towards the destruction of Verezzi, the feeble-minded painter, dramatist and dancer, who believes he is God's messenger and, supposedly inspired by higher powers, makes a mess of everything. Verezzi is a man with visions, Zastrozzi is "the master of discipline," as he is called in the play's title.

The play has been performed to great acclaim in Canada, United States, England, Australia and New Zealand and has been translated into French, Japanese and Portuguese. The reason that *Zastrozzi* has found such a great level of acceptance from the public is partly due to its great entertainment value as an audacious melodrama with duels, cutting and quick-witted dialogue. It is also because the play has as its subject matter the mysterious relationship between good and evil. Zastrozzi cynically calls Verezzi "The Christian. The great lover. The optimist."[4] "But," says the critic John Bemrose (*Macleans* 25th May 1987), "Verezzi's supposed virtue is entirely bogus. He is not only a coward but also deeply selfish. Symbolically, he stands for the hollowness of conventional morality, while

---

[4] Page 15, *Zastrozzi*, George F. Walker, Playwrights Co-op 1979

the killer Zastrozzi is the demonic power that such weakness and hypocrisy inevitably attract." It is this that makes Walker's *Zastrozzi* a play that also suits our times, in which—also in the words of Bemrose— "'civilised' societies of educated people murder millions of people in gas chambers and hoard weapons capable of destroying the planet. [...] Ultimately, Zastrozzi and Verezzi personify warring halves of the contemporary mind." (*Macleans*, 25th May 1987)

In a production of Zastrozzi, which he directed ten years after the play's premiere, it was important to Walker not to lean too heavily on earlier productions in which many of the comical elements, which were very important to him, were not played to their best advantage.

Themes
- Crime and revenge
- The struggle between good and evil
- The meaning of art
- Sense versus madness

Some other plays
Available from Playwrights Guild of Canada:
- *Prince of Naples*
- *Sacktown*

Available from University of Toronto Press:
- *Rumours of our Death* (in *Canadian Theatre Review*)

Available from Talonbooks:
- *The Art of War* (in *Shared Anxiety*)
- *Bagdad Saloon*
- *Beautiful City*
- *Better Living*
- *Beyond Mozambique* (in *Somewhere Else*)
- *Criminals in Love* (in *Shared Anxiety*)
- *Escape from Happiness* (in *Shared Anxiety*)
- *Filthy Rich* (in *The Power Plays*)
- *Gossips* (in *The Power Plays*)
- *Heaven*
- *Love & Anger* (in *East End Plays*)
- *Suburban Motel*
- *Theatre of the Film Noir* (in *Shared Anxiety*)
- *Tough* (in *Shared Anxiety*)

Some Other Voices
Brief Summaries

CAIRNS, Glen: *Danceland* (1994)

A Canadian play about a 1930's jazz duo whose marriage is falling apart, until they meet two extraordinary characters at a famous dancehall called Danceland, in Saskatchewan, who really tear their world apart.

CARLEY, Dave: *The Edible Woman* (2000)

A black comedy set in Toronto in the mid-sixties. It is based on Margaret Atwood's novel published in 1969. In this play, Marian's life seems to be perfect: a good job, interesting friends and a handsome fiancé. But slowly her world starts slipping out of focus and, instead of consuming, Marian begins identifying with the things consumed.

CHAN, Marty: *Mom, Dad, I'm Living with a White Girl* (1995)

The focus of this play is an assimilated Asian-Canadian family in a small town. A Chinese son must tell his parents that he has moved in with his white girlfriend. In a counter-narrative, the play explodes Asian stereotypes in a B-movie spoof called "Wrath of the Yellow Claw."

CHISLETT, Anne: *Quiet in the Land* (1981)

Yock brings about a crisis in his Amish community by enlisting in the First World War.

CLARK, Sally: *Jehanne of the Witches* (1989)

Christianity vs. Paganism provides the backdrop for this play-within-a-play centering on the relationship between Joan of Arc and the reputed mass murderer Gilles de Rais (Bluebeard).

DEY, Claudia: *The Gwendolyn Poems* (2002)

Nominated for the 2002 Governor General's Literary Award. A lush re-imagining of the life of legendary Canadian poet, Gwendolyn MacEwen.

FRÉCHETTE, Carole: *Carole Fréchette: Three Plays*

Translated by John Murrell. Winner of the 2002 Siminovitch prize for a playwright in mid-career. *The Four Lives of Marie*: Nominated for Nine Dora Awards, Winner of a Chalmers Award for outstanding new play, and Winner of the Governor General's Literary Award, 1995. *Elisa's Skin*: Nominated for the Governor General's Literary Award 1998. *Seven Days in the Life of Simon Labrosse*: Nominated for the governor General's Literary Award 1999. Fréchette is a Québec-based playwright whose works combine an almost archaic lyricism with contemporary subject matter.

GOW, David: *Cherry Docs* (1998)
A neo-Nazi skinhead is charged with murder, and Legal Aid has assigned him to a Jewish lawyer. Over the cause of developing a defence for the skinhead, the lawyer is forced to examine the limits of his own liberalism, and the demons underlying it.

CAMPBELL, Maria/**GRIFFITHS**, Linda: *The Book of Jessica* (1986)
A half-breed woman embarks on a spiritual journey. Her past is played out within a ceremony by Bear, Coyote, Wolverine and Unicorn.

GIBSON, Florence: *Belle* (2000)
An extraordinary story of two recently freed slaves, husband and wife, journeying to the north in search of a new life. When they encounter a white woman working for the suffrage movement, they become entwined in the social upheaval that epitomizes post Civil War America.

HEALEY, Michael: *Plan B* (2002)
High level meetings to negotiate the departure of Québec from Canada are charged by personal impulses toward seduction and betrayal, union and division, intimacy and distance.

HUNTER, Maureen: *Beautiful Lake Winnipeg* (1990)
A man accompanies his fiancée to her lakeside cabin, only to find her ex-husband waiting for them. A riveting tongue-in-cheek tale about adults who play dangerous games.

---: *Transit of Venus* (1992)
France, 1760. Astronomer Guillaume le Gentil sets sail for India. He leaves behind three women: his mother, his housekeeper and his young fiancée. Hoping to chart the transit of Venus, le Gentil travels half the world – only to finally take the measure of his own heart.

---: *Atlantis* (1996)
The story of a love affair between a Greek woman and a Canadian man, set on the island of Santorini, and told in a style that is both erotic and mystical.

JOHNSTON, Simon: *Running Dog, Paper Tiger* (1997)
Set in Hong Kong in 1967 when Communist Chinese riots rocked the stability of the British colony. A mixed-race family is forced to choose between loyalty to their British roots or to their race.

LILL, Wendy: *Glace Bay Miner's Museum* (1995)

Based on the novel by Sheldon Currie, this is the story of an ill-fated love between a wandering musician/social idealist and a Cape Breton coal miner's daughter whose dreams are reawakened by their passion.

MACLENNAN, Michael Lewis: *Beat the Sunset* (1993)

Ten years after a shattering crisis, Adam and Sacha meet again. Together they forge a relationship which transforms them both. Weaving themes of memory, AIDS, a mother's love and the history of epidemics, this is an explosive, life-affirming work about the discovery of intimacy.

---: *Grace* (1996)

Charts the lives of six people in the course of one day, as their paths intersect and affect one another. The play investigates synchronicity, fate and affection while exploring what it means to achieve the grace of meaningful human connections between strangers in public urban places.

---: *The Shooting Stage* (2002)

The title is a play on words: "shooting" as in cameras and guns (and even, perhaps, the adolescent growth spurt, seen by some as erotic in the extreme). In his multi-layered script, MacLennan explores the bullying and gay bashing that teenage boys indulge in as they struggle to sort out their sexuality. And he tears the scabs off dysfunctional father/son or surrogate father/son relationships.

MARTINI, Clem: *Illegal Entry* (1995)

Three teens escape from a group home for young offenders intending to head out to the west coast and freedom. To raise funds for this ennobling enterprise they attempt to burglarize a house. Things take an unexpected turn when they suddenly find themselves trapped in the garage. One of them happens upon an electric sander and they decide to sand their way to freedom.

MCCLELLAND GLASS, Joanna: *If We Are Women* (1994)

Looks back through three generations of mothers and daughters, tracing the hopes and disappointments, the loves and losses, and the bonds and distances.

MOUAWAD, Wajdi: *Wedding Day at the Cro-Magnons'* (1994)
Set in war-torn Beirut. A family decides to go ahead with the marriage of their only daughter despite the world crumbling around them, despite the mother's unhappiness and the father's violence, despite the mental deficiency of the youngest son and the absence of the oldest son, and above all, despite the fact that the bridegroom doesn't exist.

---: *Alphonse* (1998)
Little Alphonse has disappeared. Everyone is looking for him: his parents, his friends, the police. Meanwhile, Alphonse is strolling around the countryside, inventing the fabulous adventures of Pierre-Paul-René.

---: *Tideline* (2002) (French title *Littoral* (1999) Winner of the Governor General's Literary Award)
Wilfrid learns about the death of his father in the middle of the night. The father, whom he had never known, had abandoned him at his birth; his birth which killed his mother. The son now discovers his father through letters which his parent wrote to him but never posted. The voyage Wilfrid undertakes with the mortal remains of the deceased to bury his father in his native country redefines for him his ideas of his own identity, of life and death, and of people in general.

O'REILLY, James: *Act of God* (1999)
On the eve of his 40th birthday Jim is in the dentist's chair for the first time in 20 years. As he counts backwards from 100 and the anaesthetic kicks in, his mind wanders back through a childhood spent on the road and an incomprehensible act of God that changed everything – being struck by lightning.

PIATIGORSKY, Anton: *The Kabbalistic Psychoanalysis of Adam R. Tzaddik* (1998)
Psychic conflicts take on mythological significance, in a play about a young man's obsession with a sacred Jewish text. The play chronicles the psychoanalysis of Adam Tzaddik as he and his doctor uncover the root of Adam's denials of Jesus.

---: *The Offering* (2000)
Drawing on the classic tales of biblical patriarchs, *The Offering* explores timeless problems of communication between fathers and sons. In a trio of episodes, the play follows four generations of a single family as it struggles towards an ambiguous triumph.

QUAN, Betty: *Mother Tongue* (1994)
>The play is about family loyalties, youthful desires and generational and cultural differences. It weaves together Cantonese, English and American sign language. (Scirocco Drama)

ROBINSON, Mansel: *Colonial Tongues* (1993)
>In a small Northern Ontario town in 1967, Edna Barrett finds her family in moral jeopardy. In 1997, her youngest son returns home – to a ghost town.

SAFDIE, Oren: *Private Jokes, Public Places* (2001)
>On the surface *Private Jokes, Public Places* is a contemporary play about a rather straightforward architecture thesis, a modern urban swimming pool. Margaret, an attractive young student, presents her original design to her professors. But when the placid calm is rollicked by waves of dissent about architectural theories, sexual roles and more, egos clash and a pool is no longer just a pool.

STETSON, Kent: *The Harps of God* (1997)
>This play poses the question, what does it take to survive? How does an individual find the will to survive in a hopeless and absurd scenario?

These summaries are taken from:
• PUC Catalogue of Canadian Plays 2000
• Québec Plays in Translation, CEAD 1998
• the back covers of the respective plays
• the Internet

Note: With very few exceptions, all plays in this book, including those listed under "Further Recommendations" may be ordered from:
orders@playwrightscanada.com
and may be found at:
www.playwrightsguild.ca

—•— Afterword: After Words —•—

As Jerry Wasserman observes in his Introduction to this handbook, the plays that Albert-Reiner Glaap chooses to include admirably indicate the range and vitality of contemporary Canadian playwriting. Like all such compendiums, however, his selection is noteworthy also for what it omits – which leaves it vulnerable to the types of criticism that usually attend such projects. Inevitably, some will question its omissions – for example, work by Robert Lepage. The peripatetic director from Québec City whose innovative creations with two Québécois companies, Theatre Repère and Ex Machina, tour the globe so extensively that they represent the best known theatre to issue from Canada during the last two decades.

While it would be counter-productive simply to identify titles that Albert-Reiner Glaap could include, it remains useful to speculate why some are omitted – not to "second guess" Albert Glaap's decisions but to suggest contexts that affected them. Occlusions from a compendium are notable not only in themselves but also for the cultural and aesthetic cir-cumstances they circumscribe. In this instance, a consideration of some of the titles that aren't included facilitates observations about contemporary Canadian theatre that are different from those allowed by Albert-Reiner Glaap's selection.

A brief return to the work of Robert Lepage and his collaborators (chief of whom is Marie Brassard) illustrates this point. Although some of Lepage's creations are published in both French and English (*Polygraph* for example, and *The Seven Streams of the River Ota*), most are unavailable in print. Watching one of Lepage's highly imagistic productions helps to explain why. Besides using actors in ways that emphasize their physicality, Lepage incorporates film and digital technology into his productions, along with highly stylized approaches to lighting, music and sound. Ultimately his approach makes both scenography and *mise en scène* more important to his work than spoken text. Put simply: Lepage's directorial strategies in productions such as *Tectonic Plates* and *Needles and Opium* do not transfer well to the page – or, more precisely, they do not *read* well as "scripts." This applies to work by other Canadian and Québécois artists who privilege scenographic and directorial effects over literary technique. Frequently, their approach leads to a fusion of theatre and dance that not only defies written documentation but defeats genre categorization as well. Certainly this is the case with work created by Gilles Maheu, artistic director of Carbone 14, another Québécois company that tours regularly from its base in Montreal. To create such well-known pieces as *Le Rail, Le Dortoir*, and *Le Forêt*, Maheu functions as much as a choreographer as a director, developing performance texts in which physical, visual and aural vocabularies dominate the word. In *Le Dortoir*, for example, his actors mobilize movable metal beds in frenetic scenes of stylized activity that suggest the turbulence that can follow adolescent desire when it is freed from social constraints.

Like Gilles Maheu, other Québécois directors such as Jean Asselin and Paula de Vasconcelos (Le Théâtre pigeons international) work with artists whose training cuts across the performance spectrum; rarely do their ensembles include a playwright. As a result, the productions they create are better considered varieties of performance than genres of literature. At their most extreme, these productions have more in common with the scenic wizardry of *Le Cirque du soleil*, currently Quebec's best known theatrical export, than with the texts included in this handbook, plays whose theatricality inheres in their ability to marshal words to stimulate ideas and emotions primarily through the development of characters in conflict. Indubitably, the dramatic potential of the plays in this volume is best realized in productions that utilize many of the same material elements as their imagistic and physical counterparts; but it also can be ascertained through a careful reading of their scripts.

The work of DNA Theatre, a Toronto company founded by Hillar Liitoja in 1982, further illustrates why this is not the case with imagistic productions. While some of Liitoja's creations from the late 1980s and early 1990s utilize scripted text (most notably, *This is What Happens in Orangeville* and *The Last Supper*), his recent productions explore the theories and techniques of Antonin Artaud almost to the exclusion of words. In his piece titled *Phalanx*, for example, a wedge of actors leads a mobile audience through public streets and parks in a rigorous alternation of physical regimentation and abandon. This work constitutes the extremity of the non-literary theatre created by contemporary Canadian artists. Although words still retain interest for most of these artists, rarely are they essential. Indeed, the exploration of extra-verbal possibilities fervently replaces them as a priority.

Interestingly, some of the artists who create such work are writers as well as directors. Daniel MacIvor, for example, a playwright and performer whose monologue, *House*, is included here, investigates the theatrical possibilities of movement in plays such as *2-2 Tango* and *Jump*, as well as of lighting in *The Soldier Dreams* and *Monster*. Although his collaborations with Daniel Brooks, a playwright/performer best known as a director, usually incorporate spoken text, they often foreground extended sequences of music and movement as well. Invariably the sequences create *coups de théâtre* that overwhelm the spoken word in their intensity. This effect also applies to work created by Jacquie P. A. Thomas and Theatre Gargantuan, another Toronto company. The title of the company's best known creation, *Raging Dreams: Into the Visceral*, indicates Thomas' pursuit of a theatricality that cannot be achieved by the use of techniques aimed solely at intellectual and/or emotional response.

The exploration of theatrical vocabularies that exist before or after words leads many Canadian theatre artists to stretch and tease the conventions of literary form as well as to surround words with extra-linguistic devices. Both approaches direct the audience's attention away from semantic significance towards the elements of performance. One Yellow Rabbit, a company based in Calgary, annually highlights the best of this work in a festival titled High Performance Rodeo. The collaborations of Blake Brooker, Michael Green and Denise Clarke, all co-founders of the company, consistently demonstrate the "high theatricality" that can attend the performance of words approached as matter, not meaning – that is, as sounds which stimulate sensual more than cognitive effect.

In this regard, the work of One Yellow Rabbit parallels creations by Théâtre Ubu, a Montréal company which, as its name implies, evokes artistic principles espoused by Alfred Jarry, the theatrical iconoclast whose plays scandalized French society at the turn of the century. In works like *Oulipo Show* and *Merz Opéra*, Théâtre Ubu reduces verbal expression to "pure sound" by abstracting words and mechanizing movement to a point beyond logic. Such "pataphysical" performance challenges bourgeois notions of acceptable theatre as well as the structures of thought signified by the "sensible" use of words. Like the work of the Futurists and Dadaists to which it often is comported, such work frequently attempts to represent social and political realities that remain marginal in dominant modes of expression.

It is no coincidence that the historical precedents for contemporary Canadian theatre, even its most marginal forms, emanate primarily from Europe. The shift from Europe to Asia that illustrates changes in Canadian immigration patterns typical of the late 20th century is not yet represented in Canadian theatre by the significant emergence of non-European theatrical processes and forms – a situation that such explicitly multicultural theatres such as Teesri Duniya, a company founded in Montréal during the late 1980s, aims to redress. As Jerry Wasserman points out, however, the representation of Canada's First Nations is increasing in Canadian theatre, a fact that the inclusion of plays by Daniel David Moses, Tomson Highway and Drew Hayden Taylor in this volume substantiates.

Other types of performance-based theatre created by First Nations artists parallel the success of these plays. *Moonlodge* by Margo Kane, a Vancouver writer and performer, is one of the best known. Presented as a ritual in which the audience is invited to complete a circle initiated by the performer, the piece suggests a ceremony where, again, words cease to function as linguistic signs. In this instance the emptying words of intellectuals signification serves a different end than in pataphysical performance: it allows them to function as spiritual conduits. In performances by Kane and artists creating similar work, theatre potentially transforms into a metaphysical experience, a time and place of spiritual recuperation. Here, chant and incantation function like Buddhist mantras to transport both performers and audience into a non-material dimension.

More Eurocentric in their approach to words as sensory stimuli are Mump and Smoot, two Toronto-based performers whose grotesque clown-work follows the tradition of French *buffon*. In pieces such as *Something and Caged*, Michael Kennard (Mump) and John Turner (Smoot) create a unique form of savage silliness in part by garbling words beyond recognition, reducing them to distended squeaks and grunts that suggest emotional states without signifying specific meanings. Wearing garish costumes as well as makeup exaggerated to the point of mask, Mump and Smoot create vivid spectacles in which slapstick physical display complements incomprehensible utterance to complete bizarre scenarios that are as visually horrific as they are humorous.

Highly visual performances like these are better documented by photography than words which explains why work by Mump and Smoot, despite its originality and popularity, is absent from this collection. Other Canadian creations that are equally, if not more, spectacular in their use of visual techniques warrant mention in this regard for, increasingly, many audiences and critics view them as pre-eminent examples of this approach to theatre. Not surprisingly, many of these rely not only on masks and mime but also on puppetry and other movement forms that, though stylized, are not perceived as dance.

In the 1990s, the foremost example of mask work to emerge in Canada is *The Number 14* which, like other productions mentioned here, has toured both inside and out of Canada to critical and popular acclaim. Conceived by Wayne Specht of Vancouver's Axis Theatre in 1992 and subsequently developed in collaboration with director Roy Surette at Touchstone Theatre, another Vancouver company, *The Number 14* uses a six-person cast to perform more than 60 characters who get on and off a bus (the number 14) as it cuts a swath across the socio-economic diversity of present-day Vancouver. Employing masks, mime, dance, acrobatics and clown, the actors offer a virtuoso display of comic technique in the two-hour show that opts for picaresque variety over dramatic cohesion. While the show uses spoken text, it minimizes its significance by reducing its contribution to character creation. Psychological portraiture is replaced by sociological sketch, communicated not only by the use of evocative masks and costumes but also by the boldly stylized physical style that aims to represent types rather than individuals. *The Number 14* appeals to children and adults alike, which often is the case with shows created by the Mermaid Theatre as well, despite its primary commitment to theatre for young audiences (TYA). Situated in Windsor, Nova Scotia, Mermaid has built its reputation over three decades by creating highly visual work that represents local legends through the integration of puppet forms with performance by masked actors and live musicians. Although the company now has expanded its repertoire by creating work that uses more traditional theatrical forms, it continues to rely primarily on puppets and mime, as does Ronnie Burkett, a writer and performer from Medicine Hat, Alberta, who, in the productions he creates for his Theatre of Marionettes, presents a unique performance experience that has won international acclaim. More than any of the examples of contemporary Canadian theatre cited above, the theatre of Ronnie Burkett relies on scripts that adhere to conventions established by traditional dramatic forms. For productions like *Tinka's New Dress*, *Old Friends* and *Street of Blood*, Burkett writes plays in which the structural sophistication of incident and plot carefully complements the clever use of characterization and dialogue. The fact remains, however, that besides making his puppets, Burkett openly manipulates them in performance, ventriloquizing his witty texts into his marionettes with techniques that foreground his role as puppeteer. While Burkett's polished presentations never devalue his scripts, they inevitably direct the audience's attention to the performer who delivers them. In part, the theatrical magic of Burkett's theatre ensues from this revelation of theatrical process. By allowing the audience to watch him manipulate his puppets, Burkett invites them to consider the relationship between playwriting and performance in his work, and to marvel at how the effect of the former depends on the skill of the latter.

The work of Montreal's Le Théâtre de la marmaille, another company devoted to TYA, often has the same effect though for different reasons, as one of its best known productions, *Terre Promise/Terra Promessa* illustrates. Developed in collaboration with Teatro Dell'Angelo of Turin, Italy, *Promised Land* eschews spoken text altogether, using mime, music, costume and innovative scenography to create a stunning visual narrative that traces the progress of a stone from pre-history to the present-day through a variety of fictional and historic incidents. Although words are unnecessary to its overall effect, their exclusion arguably diminishes the importance of the topics that the piece addresses, opening it to accusations of intellectual obscurity and oversimplification.

The reliance on physical metaphor and visual metonymy in the work of Le Théâtre de la marmaille is consistent with most of the work cited above. The criticism that much of this work is intellectually immature frequently attends the delight that greets its performance. Words, or, to be more accurate, the imaginative use of words in the service of drama, still command the greatest respect of most people interested in Canadian theatre – if only because words are considered tantamount to thought, and thought is still the most acceptable goal of art. What can theatre achieve when it moves beyond words? The question interrogates not only the function of words in the theatre but of theatre in society.

The fact that Le Théâtre de la marmaille developed *Promised Land* in collaboration with an Italian company, with the specific aim of touring the show to international theatre festivals in a variety of countries, is important in this regard. Frequently, word-based theatre is treated less than enthusiastically by people who program international festivals, for they recognize that a script in a foreign language, no matter how brilliantly it is produced, still can present problems for a local audience. As a result, such programmers often develop a predilection for productions that are more visual than linguistic in their construction, which invariably leads them to privilege performance-based creations over literary ones. This is lamentable for it contributes to the misunderstandings, if not ill will, that can separate artists' intent on producing word-based theatre from those more interested in alternative performance forms.

If this Afterword helps to alleviate such misunderstandings, it achieves its purpose. Canadian theatre artists are best served by collaborating in as many forms as possible, not by competing for the prominence of one over another. As this handbook proves, words continue to invigorate Canadian and Québécois theatre. For some readers, it may be surprising to learn that, after words, other forms of performance flourish equally well across the country.

Bob Wallace
Robarts Chair for Canadian Studies 1998-1999
York University, Toronto

Cumulative list of nominees for the
Governor General's Literary Awards
—•— Drama / Théâtre —•—
Liste cumulative des œuvres en lice pour
les Prix Littéraires du Gouverneur Géneral

•1981•
Blood Relations Sharon Pollock (NeWest Press)
Straight Ahead and Blind Dancers Charles Tidler (Playwrights Canada)
Theatre of the Film Noir George F. Walker (Playwrights Canada)
C'était avant la guerre à l'anse à Gilles Marie Laberge (VLB Éditeur)
Vie et mort du Roi Boiteux Jean-Pierre Ronfard (Leméac)

•1982•
Billy Bishop Goes to War John Gray (Talonbooks)
Clay Lawrence Jeffery (Playwrights Canada)
Jennie's Story Betty Lambert (Playwrights Canada)
Ha ha! ... Réjean Ducharme (Éditions Lacombe)
Avec L'hiver qui s'en vient Marie Laberge (VLB Éditeur)
... Quand j'y ai dit ca ... à parti à rire Léo Lévesque (Éditions
    coopératives Albert Saint-Martin)
La terre est trop courte, Violette Leduc Jovette Marchessault (Les Éditions
    de la Pleine Lune)

•1983•
Quiet in the Land Anne Chislett (Coach House Press)
La passion de Juliette Michelle Allen (Éditions Leméac)
26 bis, impasse du Colonel Foisy René-Daniel Dubois (Éditions Leméac)
Syncope René Gingras (Éditions Leméac)

•1984•
The Canadian Brothers or The Prophecy Fulfilled James Reaney (Irwin)
A Letter to My Son George Ryga (Turnstone)
White Biting Dog Judith Thompson (Playwrights Canada)
Ne blâmez jamais les Bédouins René-Daniel Dubois (Leméac)
Les Transporteurs de monde Gilbert Dupuis (Éditions coop. de la Mêlée)
Pleurer pour rire Marcel Sabourin (VLB Éditeur)
Albertine en cinq temps Michel Tremblay (Leméac)

•1985•
Salt-water Moon David French (Playwrights Canada)
War Babies (in *Willful Acts: Five Plays*) Margaret Hollingsworth (The
    Coach House Press)

Gone the Burning Sun Ken Mitchell (Playwrights Canada)
Criminals in Love George F. Walker (Playwrights Canada)
La poupée de Pélopia Michel Marc Bouchard (Leméac)
Chandeleur Francine Noel (VLB Éditeur)
***Duo pour voix obstinées* Maryse Pelletier (VLB Éditeur)**

•1986•
Odd Jobs Frank Moher (Playwrights Canada)
Doc Sharon Pollock (Playwrights Canada)
Papers Allan Stratton (Playwrights Canada)
Fragments d'une letter d'adieu lus par des géologues Normand Chaurette
    (Éditions Leméac)
Les nouilles Yves Desgagnés et Louise Roy (Éditions Leméac)
***La visite des sauvages* Anne Legault (VLB Éditeur)**
Le Titanic Jean-Pierre Ronfard (Éditions Leméac)

•1987•
Prague (Winner) John Krizanc (Playwrights Canada)
The Occupation of Heather Rose Wendy Lill (NeWest Press)
Walt and Roy Michael D.C. McKinlay (Playwrights Canada)
Whiskey Six Cadenza Sharon Pollock (NeWest Press)
La Nuit des p'tits couteaux Suzanne Aubry (Éditions Leméac)
**Un oiseau vivant dans la gueule Jeanne-Mance Delisle (Éditions de la
    pleine lune)**
Oublier Marie Laberge (VLB Éditeur)
La vrai monde? Michel Tremblay (Éditions Leméac)

•1988•
Skin from *Skin and Liars* Dennis Foon (Playwrights Canada)
The Rez Sisters Tomson Highway (Fifth House)
Footprints on the Moon Maureen Hunter (Blizzard Publishing)
***Nothing Sacred* George F. Walker (Coach House Press)**
Le Syndrome de Cézanne Normand Canac-Marquis (Éditions Les Herbes
    Rouges)
***Le Chien* Jean marc Dalpé (Éditions Pris de Parole)**
Oui ou non Marie-Francine Hébert (VLB Éditeur)
Déjà l'agonie Marco Micone (Éditions de l'Hexagone)
Le Déversoir des larmes André Ricard (Guérin littérature)

•1989•
Dry Lips Oughta Move to Kapuskasing Tomson Highway (Fifth House
    Publishers)
Tamara John Krizanc (Stoddart Publishing)
***The Other Side of the Dark* Judith Thompson (Coach House Press)**
Les Muses orphelines Michel Marc Bouchard (Leméac)

La Femme d'intérieur Robert Claing (VLB Éditeur)
Mademoiselle Rouge **Michel Garneau (VLB Éditeur)**

•1990•

Black Friday? Audrey Butler (Women's Press)
Goodnight Desdemona (Good Morning Juliet) **Ann-Marie MacDonald (Coach House Press)**
Scientific Americans John Mighton (Playwrights Canada Press)
Love and Anger George F. Walker (Coach House Press)
Le Troisième fils du professeur Yourolov René-Daniel Dubois (**Leméac Éditeur**)
L'Île de la Demoiselle Anne Hébert (Éditions du Boréal/Le Seuil)
Le Voyage magnifique d'Emily Carr **Jovette Marchessault (Leméac Éditeur)**

•1991•

The Trial of Judith K. Sally Clark (Playwrights Canada)
Where is Kabuki? Don Druick (Playwrights Canada)
The Darling Family Linda Griffiths (Blizzard Publishing)
Amigo's Blue Guitar **Joan MacLeod (Blizzard Publishing)**
Coyote City Daniel David Moses (Williams-Wallace Publishers)
La maison cassée Victor-Lévy Beaulieu (Éditions Stanké)
L'Histoire de l'oie Michel Marc Bouchard (Leméac Éditeur)
La répétition Dominic Champagne (VLB Éditeur)
Mon oncle Marcel qui vague près du métro Berri **Gilbert Dupuis (Éditions de l'Hexagone)**
Conte du jour et de la nuit Suzanne Lebeau (Leméac Éditeur)

•1992•

The Noam Chomsky Lectures Daniel Brooks and Guillermo Verdecchia (Coach House Press)
Writing With Our Feet Dave Carley (Blizzard Publishing)
Possible Worlds and A Short History of Night **John Mighton (Playwrights Canada Press)**
Lion in the Streets Judith Thompson (Coach House Press)
Serpent in the Night Sky Dianne Warren (Playwrights Canada Press)
La cité interdite Dominic Champagne (VLB Éditeur)
Anna Robert Claing (Éditions du Boréal)
Pierre ou la consolation Marie Laberge (Éditions du Boréal)
Les petits orteils **Louis-Dominique Lavigne (VLB Éditeur)**
Tu faisais comme un appel Marthe Mercure (Éditions Les Herbes rouges)

•1993•

House Humans Daniel MacIvor (Coach House Press)
The Saints and Apostles Raymond Storey (Playwrights Canada Press)
***Fronteras Americanas* Guillermo Verdecchia (Coach House Press)**
Glenn David Young (Coach House Press)
***Celle-là* Daniel Danis (Leméac Éditeur)**
Petit Monstre Jasmine Dubé (Leméac Éditeur)
Kushapatshikan Gilbert Dupuis (VLB Éditeur)

•1994•

If We Are Women Joanna McClelland Glass (Playwrights Canada Press)
All Fall Down Wendy Lill (Talonbooks)
Whale Riding Weather Bryden MacDonald (Talonbooks)
***The Ends of the Earth* Morris Panych (Talonbooks)**
Morgane Michelle Allen (Éditions du Boréal)
Histoires à mourir d'amour Yvan Bienvenue (Éditions Les Herbes rouges)
***French Town* Michel Ouellette (Éditions du Nordir)**
Si tu meurs, je te tue Claude Poissant (Éditions Les Herbes rouges)
Cinq études Jean-Pierre Ronfard (Leméac Éditeur)

•1995•

Poor Super Man: A Play with Captions Brad Fraser (NeWest Press)
Miracle Mother Deborah Kimmett (Scirocco Drama)
The Hope Slide – Little Sister Joan MacLeod (Coach House Press)
***Three in the Back, Two in the Head* Jason Sherman (Playwrights Canada
    Press)**
Some Assembly Required Eugene Stickland (Coteau Books)
Lucky Lady Jean Marc Dalpé (Éditions du Boréal/Prise de Parole)
***Le Quatre Morts de Marie* Carole Fréchette (Éditions Les Herbes rouges)**
Contes d'enfants réels Suzanne Lebeau (VLB Éditeur)
Marina, le dernier rose aux joues Michèle Magny (Leméac Éditeur/Actes
    Sud-Papiers)

•1996•

The Glace Bay Miners' Museum Wendy Lill (Talonbooks)
The Little Years John Mighton (Playwrights Canada Press)
Mad Boy Chronicle Michael O'Brien (Playwrights Canada Press)
Mother Tongue Betty Quan (Scirocco Drama)
***The Monument* Colleen Wagner (Playwrights Canada Press)**
***Le Passage de l'Indiana* Normand Chaurette (Leméac Éditeur/Actes Sud-
    Papiers)**
Salvador Suzanne Lebeau (VLB Éditeur)
Alphonse Wajdi Mouawad (Leméac Editeur)

•1997•

Atlantis Maureen Hunter (Scirroco Drama/J. Gordon Shillingford
    Publishing)
High Life Lee MacDougall (Scirroco Drama/J. Gordon Shillingford
    Publishing)
***fareWel* Ian Ross (Scirroco Drama/J. Gordon Shillingford Publishing)**
Reading Hebron Jason Sherman (Playwrights Canada Press)
Sled Judith Thompson (Playwrights Canada Press)
***Dits et Inédits* Yvan Bienvenue (Dramaturges Éditeurs)**
La Bonne Femme Jasmine Dubé (Leméac Éditeur)
Une tache sur la lune Marie-Line Laplante (Dramaturges Éditeurs)
L'Insomnie Robert Marinier P(rise de parole)
Ogre-Cornemuse Larry Tremblay (Éditions Lansman)

•1998•

Selkirk Avenue Bruce McManus (Nuage Editions)
Not Spain Richard Sanger (Playwrights Canada Press)
***Harlem Duet* Djanet Sears (Scirroco Drama/J. Gordon Shillingford
    Publishing)**
Sandra Shamas: A Trilogy of Performances Sandra Shamas (Mercury
    Press)
Inexpressible Island David Young (Scirroco Drama/J. Gordon Shillingford
    Publishing)
***15 secondes* Francois Archambault (Leméac Éditeur)**
Motel Hélène Serge Boucher (Dramaturges Éditeurs)
Le Bain des raines Olivier Choinière (Dramaturges Éditeurs)
Le Peau d'Élisa Carole Fréchette (Leméac Éditeur/Actes Sud)
L'Ogrelet Suzanne Lebeau (Lanctôt Éditeur)

•1999•

***The Drawer Boy* Michael Healey (Playwrights Canada Press)**
Corker Wendy Lill (Talonbooks)
Marion Bridge Daniel MacIvor (Talonbooks)
Beating Heart Cadaver Colleen Murphy (Playwrights Canada Press)
Still the Night Theresa Tova (Scirroco Drama/J. Gordon Shillingford
    Publishing)
***Il n'y a que l'amour* Jean Marc Dalpé (Éditions Prise de parole)**
Les Sept Jours de Simon Labrosse Carole Fréchette (Leméac Éditeur/Actes
    Sud-Papiers)
D'Avila René Gingras (Éditions Lansman)
Encore une fois, si vous permettez Michel Tremblay (Leméac Éditeur)

•2000•

Consecrated Ground George Boyd (Blizzard Publishing)
Elizabeth Rex Timothy Findley (Blizzard Publishing)
Alien Creature Linda Griffiths (Playwrights Canada Press)
Monster Daniel MacIvor and Daniel Brooks (Scirroco Drama/J. Gordon
　　Shillingford Publishing)
It's All True Jason Sherman (Playwrights Canada Press)
Crime contre l'humanité Geneviève Billette (Leméac Éditeur)
24 Poses Serge Boucher (Dramaturges Éditeurs)
L'Arche de Noémie Jasmine Dubé (Lanctôt Éditeur)
Littoral Wajdi Mouawad (Leméac Éditeur/Actes Sud)
Le petit dragon, suivi de La balade de Fannie et Carcassonne Lise
　　Vaillancourt (Les éditions Lansman)

•2001•

Monsieur d'Eon Mark Brownell (Playwrights Canada Press)
A Three Martini Lunch Clem Martini (Red Deer Press)
Building Jerusalem Michael Redhill (Playwrights Canada Press)
An Acre of Time: The Play Jason Sherman (Playwrights Canada Press)
The Harps of God Kent Stetson (Playwrights Canada Press)
Code 99 Francois Archambault (Dramaturges Éditeurs)
Un Autre Monde Réjane Charpentier (Lanctôt Éditeur)
Le Petit Köchel Normand Chaurette (Leméac Éditeur/Actes Sud)
«Requiem», dans Requiem suivi de Fausse route Michel Ouellette (Le
　　Nordir)

•2002•

The Gwendolyn Poems Claudia Dey (Playwrights Canada Press)
Je me souviens Lorena Gale (Talonbooks)
Unity (1918) Kevin Kerr (Talonbooks)
The Shooting Stage Michael Lewis MacLennan (Playwrights Canada
　　Press)
Le Langue-à-Langue des chiens Daniel Danis (L'Arche Éditeur de roche)
Jean et Béatrice Carole Fréchette (Leméac Éditeur/Actes Sud)
Rêves Wajdi Mouawad (Leméac Éditeur/Actes Sud)
L'Hôtel des Horizons Reynald Robinson (Dramaturges Éditeurs)
Le rire de la mer Pierre-Michel Tremblay (Lanctôt éditeur)

—•— Playwrights Guild of Canada —•—
(PGC)

I recently saw a good production of an American play at a summer festival in Nova Scotia. After the show, a few of us stood around under the stars in the open air lobby, beverages in hands, discussing the play. It's so American, someone said. Isn't it though? Someone else agreed. Can't you just see an American audience just loving it? Such an American play.

That's probably a good sign, said a well-known Atlantic playwright, nodding towards the discussion. Yes, I said, because if we can identify this as an American play, and we know it is nothing like what we do, then – there must be such a thing as a Canadian play, we said together.

At the risk of seeming to once again identify ourselves in relation to that Goliath to the south of us, I believe it is possible to say that there is a Canadian play.

So much has changed. When I started to attend theatre, I would have been hard pressed to find even one Canadian play on any stage, had it even occurred to me to look. Then we went through the difficult period of fighting the perception Canadian play = bad play, when world-class theatre plays meant Shakespeare and Ibsen and Chekhov and Brecht and Miller and Beckett. And then something happened, and Canadian plays began to gain respect, Canadian audiences began to hunger for Canadian voices, for our own stories, and we began to see Canadian plays on Canadian stages.

Now there is a Canadian play, and it has a distinctive voice, whether it comes from the north, an urban centre, the prairies, the west coast or the east. And the Canadian play is not just not American, not only not British, it is Canadian, it is in a voice that speaks to us as Canadians.

Standing on the edge of the millennium looking into the future, we cast a look over a shoulder to see where we came from, how we got here.

The first organisation created to ensure the perpetuation of Canadian voices for the stage was the Playwright Circle, formed in 1971. The Canada Council for the Arts offered support to establish a resource centre for Canadian playwriting, and in 1972, the Circle became the Playwrights Co-op and began publishing Canadian plays, and a catalogue to market them. In 1977, some Co-op members founded the Guild of Canadian Playwrights to do the other major job that playwrights needed done: contract negotiations. In 1984, the two organisations merged to become the Playwrights Union of Canada (PUC). In 2002, PUC and its publishing imprint, Playwrights Canada Press, split again, and PUC renamed itself Playwrights Guild of Canada (PGC).

Thirty years later, PGC is the source for Canadian plays and playwrights. PGC is the professional association for more than 450 playwrights who are produced on stages of this country from coast to coast, and in England, Germany, the United States, Italy, Australia and other countries around the world. The services the organisation provides to its members, to the Canadian theatre community and to the public are so many and so diverse that new members often express amazement at what we do.

For in addition to those two primary purposes—copying and distributing of scripts and contract negotiations—what we do has grown to include production and distribution of the catalogue and directory, representation at various tables on the issues of copyright and public lending right, the handling of amateur and professional rights, the lobbying of governments, the organisation of readings and workshops for members, the publication of the newsmagazine *CanPlay*, and the maintenance of a website that makes us accessible to the world.

We are the voices of Canadian theatre, from the writers who are now a part of a Canadian canon – David French and Tomson Highway and Judith Thompson, Wendy Lill and Dennis Foon and Norm Foster – to the newer kids on the block – Daniel MacIvor and David Gow and Djanet Sears and younger, newer playwrights still, writers you have not yet heard of, but you will. We are here, in the pages of the publications of the Playwrights Guild of Canada, on our website, on the curricula of our schools and universities and on the stages of this country. We are an integral and enduring part of the culture of this country. We are the playwrights of the Playwrights Guild of Canada.

Yvette Nolan (PGC)
www.playwrightsguild.ca

—•— Le Centre des auteurs dramatiques —•—
(CEAD)

For more than thirty years, the Centre des auteurs dramatiques (CEAD) has worked towards the development of new Québec theatre. Le Centre des auteurs dramatiques was founded in Montréal in 1965. Its current membership numbers close to 175 French-language playwrights. CEAD has two main objectives: to develop and to promote Québec plays and playwrights at home and abroad.

A dramaturge/literary manager at the Centre oversees a wide range of dramaturgical services and activities that include a reading and critique service, dramaturgical consultation for professional writers, "coaching" sessions, workshops, special discussion groups and public readings.

CEAD has a documentation centre with a well-stocked reference library and a circulation service of published and unpublished scripts to professional theatre companies from Canada and elsewhere.

Le Centre des auteurs dramatiques is perhaps best known outside Québec for its work in promoting Québec plays in translation through different means: showcase readings, translation workshops and playwrights' exchanges. Over the past fifteen years, CEAD has pursued these promotional activities in collaboration with organizations across Canada, in the United States, Latin America, Great Britain and other European countries.

Publications

Québec Plays in Translation is a catalogue of Québec plays available in English translation. Published in English, it includes synopses of 187 plays, their approximate running time and cast breakdowns, as well as biographic information on the playwrights. It also lists foreign language translations.

1999 Edition of Répertoire des membres du CEAD (1999 Catalogue of Québec Plays: in French only).

CEAD also publishes *Théâtre Québec*, an annual bilingual newsletter which outlines the season's most notable theatrical activities. *Théâtre Québec* is sent to professional theatre organisations in Canada and abroad.

The Resource Centre

Every day, directors, actors, students, professors, researchers, teachers, members of community theatre groups, journalists, and artistic directors from Québec and abroad use the resources offered by CEAD's Documentation Centre. The Documentation Centre houses more than 3000 published and unpublished Québec plays.

Whether you're considering a play for production or conducting research for an academic project, a trained staff member will assist you.

The Documentation Centre houses a data bank which classifies information by title, author, cast and theme. All plays are available on location and can be consulted in our Reading Room. They can also be ordered by phone or mail. Unpublished plays will be lent to anyone who purchases a lending card. Published plays can also be purchased at the Documentation Centre or ordered by mail.

The archives of the Documentation Centre include extensive files on various aspects of Québec theatre: articles on authors, production information on plays, season schedules and programmes from theatres, etc. Our archives will likely facilitate and enrich any research pertaining to Québec drama.

cead@cead.qc.ca   www.cead.qc.ca

—•— L'Association Québécoise des Auteurs Dramatiques —•—
(AQAD)

L'Association Québécoise des Auteurs Dramatiques (AQAD) is a non-profit organization. Its mission is to defend the socio-economic, moral and professional rights and interests of French and English Québec and French Canadian playwrights, librettists, adapters and translators.

Operations
Board of Directors
(2002-2004)

Président	Raymond Villeneuve
Secrétaire	Jocelyne Beaulieu
Administrateur	Yvan Bienvenue
Administratrice	Marie-Renée Charest
Administratrice	Josée La Bossière
Administrateur	Miguel Retamal

Address:
AQAD
187, rue Sainte-Catherine Est, 3e étage
Montréal (Québec)
H2X 1K8
Telephone: (514) 596-3705
Fax: (514) 596-2953
info@aqad.qc.ca
www.aqad.qc.ca

AQAD receives assistance from the Conseil des arts et des lettres du Québec as part of its Associations professionnelles d'artistes, regroupements nationaux et organismes de services programme.

—•— Selected Bibliography —•—

Anthologies

Beissel, Henry (ed.), *Cues and Entrances*, Second Edition, Vancouver: Gage Educational Publishing Company 1993.

Bessai, Diane/Kerr, Don (eds.), *NeWest Plays by Women*, Edmonton: NeWest Publishers 1987.

Bragg, Martin/Brask, Per/Surette, Roy (eds.), *7 Cannons. Plays by Mareen Hunter, Connie Gault, Wendy Lill, Linda Griffiths, Joan MacLeod, Judith Thompson and Colleen Wagner*, Toronto: Playwrights Canada Press 2000.

Brenna, Dwayne (ed.), *Scenes from Canadian Plays. From Automatic Pilot to Zastrozzi. A Selection of Dialogues*, Saskatoon: Fifth House Publishers 1989.

Filewod, Alan (ed.), *The CTR Anthology: Fifteen Plays from Canadian Theatre Review*, Toronto: University of Toronto Press 1993.

Grace, Sherrill/D'Aeth, Eve/Chalykoff, Lisa (eds.), *Staging the North: Twelve Canadian Plays*, Toronto: Playwrights Canada Press 1999.

Hamill, Tony (ed.), *The Perfect Piece. Monologues from Canadian Plays*, Toronto: Playwrights Canada Press 1990.

Hamill, Tony (ed.), *Six Canadian Plays*, Toronto: Playwrights Canada Press 1992.

Hoyes, Mima (ed.), *Contemporary Canadian Scripts*, Volume One, Scarborough: Prentice Hall Canada Inc. 1994.

Nolan, Yvette/Quan, Betty/Seremba, George Bwanika (eds.), *Beyond the Pale. Dramatic Writing from First Nations Writers & Writers of Colour*, Toronto: Playwrights Canada Press 1996.

Perkyns, Richard (ed.), *Major Plays of the Canadian Theatre 1934-1984*, Toronto: Irwin Publishing 1984.

Plant, Richard (ed.), *The Penguin Book of Modern Canadian Drama*, Vol.1, Markham: Penguin Books Canada 1984.

Ratsoy, Ginny/Hoffman, James (eds.), *Playing the Pacific Province. An Anthology of British Columbia Plays, 1967-2000*, Toronto: Playwrights Canada Press 2001.

Ravel, Aviva (ed.), *Canadian Mosaic. 6 Plays*, Toronto: Simon & Pierre 1995.

—-, *Canadian Mosaic II. 6 Plays*, Toronto: Simon & Pierre 1996.

Sears, Djanet (ed.), *Testifyin'. Contemporary African Canadian Drama*. Vol. I, Toronto: Playwrights Canada Press 2000.

Sherman, Jason (ed.), *Solo*, Toronto: Coach House Press 1994.

Wallace, Robert (ed.), *Québec Voices. Three Plays*, Toronto: Coach House Press 1986.

Wasserman, Jerry, (ed.), *Twenty Years at Play. A New Play Centre Anthology*, Vancouver: Talonbooks 1990.

—, *Modern Canadian Plays*, Vol.1, Vancouver: Talonbooks 1993.

—, *Modern Canadian Plays*, Vol.2, Vancouver: Talonbooks 1994.

Zimmerman, Cynthia (ed.), *Taking the Stage. Selections from Plays by Canadian Women*, Toronto: Playwrights Canada Press 1994.

Reference Literature

Benson, Eugene/Conolly, Leonard W. (eds.), *English-Canadian Theatre*, Toronto: Oxford University Press 1987.

—, *The Oxford Companion to Canadian Theatre*, Toronto: Oxford University Press 1989.

Brask, Per (ed.), *Contemporary Issues in Canadian Drama*, Winnipeg: Blizzard Publishing 1995.

Conolly, Leonard W. (ed.), *Canadian Drama and the Critics*, Revised Edition, Vancouver: Talonbooks 1995.

Filewod, Alan, *Collective Encounters. Documentary Theatre in English Canada*, Toronto: University of Toronto Press 1987.

Gilbert, Helen/Tompkins, Joanne, *Post-Colonial Drama. Theory, practice, politics*, London: Routledge 1996.

Glaap, Albert-Reiner/Althof, Rolf (eds.), *On-Stage and Off-Stage. English Canadian Drama in Discourse*, St. John's: Breakwater 1996.

Knowles, Paul Richard, "Culture, Economics, and Canadian Drama in the 1990s", *Anglistik. Mitteilungen des Verbandes Deutscher Anglisten* 9/2 (September 1998). Heidelberg: Carl Winter 1998.

Maufort, Marc/Bellarsi, Franca (eds.), *Siting the Other. Revisions of Marginality in Australian and English-Canadian Drama*, Brussels: P.I.E. – Peter Lang 2001.

Much, Rita (ed.), *Women on the Canadian Stage. The Legacy of Hrotsvit*, Winnipeg: Blizzard Publishing 1992.

Rubin, Don, *Canadian Theatre History. Selected Readings*, Toronto: Copp Clark Ltd. 1996.

Rudakoff, Judith (ed.), *Questionable Activities. The Best (Interviews)*, Toronto: Playwrights Canada Press 2000.

Wagner, Anton (ed.), *Contemporary Canadian Theatre. New World Visions*, Toronto: Simon & Pierre Publishing 1985.

—, *Establishing Our Boundaries: English-Canadian Theatre Criticism*, Toronto: University of Toronto Press 2000.

Wallace, Robert, *Producing Marginality. Theatre and Criticism in Canada*, Saskatoon: Fifth House Publishers 1990.

—•— Albert-Reiner Glaap – Biographical Data —•—

Glaap, Albert-Reiner, studied English Language and Literature, Latin and Philosophy at the Universities of Cologne and London (King's College), graduated from Cologne University in 1956, Dr. phil. (Cologne University 1955); taught at various schools in Germany and the USA from 1958 to 1971; Director of the Düsseldorf Teacher Training College 1971-1973; since 1973 Universitätsprofessor at Heinrich-Heine-Universität Düsseldorf; Honorary Officer of the Order of the British Empire (OBE) since 1991; board member of Deutsch-Englische Gesellschaft, Düsseldorf since 1998; member of Advisory Council of the Association for Canadian Studies in German-Speaking Countries (1994-2000).

Special fields of research: Modern English and Canadian literature, contemporary drama and theatre in England, Canada and New Zealand; the teaching of English literature at secondary school and university level; theory and practice of literary translation.

Editor of eighteen annotated editions of British, Canadian and American plays; translator of six English stage plays into German; editor of TAGS (Literary Texts for the Gymnasiale Oberstufe); co-editor of TRANSFER (Literary Translation); general editor of CSEL (Cornelsen Senior English Literature); editor of REFLECTIONS (books on the literatures in English outside Britain and the USA).

Author of books on various subjects. Most recent publications: *Onstage and Offstage. English Canadian Drama in Discourse* (1996), *Stimmen aus Kanada. 25 kanadische Dramen für deutsche Bühnen* (1997), *A 50th Birthday Tribute to Willy Martin Russell* (1997), *A French Window onto the Old World* (1999), (with Nicholas Quaintmere) *A Guided Tour Through Ayckbourn Country* (1999), *Discover... First Nations Peoples in America,* Student's Book and Teacher's Book (1999/2001), *Ronald Harwood, "Taking Sides",* annotated edition, Student's Book and Teacher's Book (1999/2000), *Drew Hayden Taylor, "Toronto at Dreamer's Rock,* annotated edition, Student's and Teacher's Book (1995/1996), *Anne Chislett, "Flippin'In",* annotated edition (2000). Author of 220 articles in different scholarly journals, theatre programmes and reference works.

—•— Albert-Reiner Glaap – Dates biographiques —•—

Glaap, Albert-Reiner; études de littérature et langue anglaises, de latin et de philosophie aux Universités de Cologne et de Londres (King's Collège) ; diplômé de l'Université de Cologne en 1956, doctorat en 1955; il a enseigné à plusieurs écoles en Allemagne et aux Etats-Unis de 1958 à 1971; directeur du séminaire de professeurs à Düsseldorf de 1971 à 1973; depuis 1973 professeur de faculté à l'Université Heinrich-Heine de Düsseldorf; officier d'honneur du Order of the British Empire (OBE) depuis 1991; membre du conseil consultatif de l'Association allemande-anglaise de Düsseldorf depuis 1998; membre du comité consultatif de l'Association d'Etudes Canadiennes dans les pays germanophones (1994-2000).

Domaines de recherche: littératures anglaise et canadienne modernes, théâtre contemporain de l'Angleterre, du Canada et de la Nouvelle-Zélande; enseignement de la littérature anglaise à l'université et au lycée ; théorie et pratique de la traduction littéraire.

Editeur de 18 éditions commentées de pièces de théâtre britanniques, canadiennes et américaines; traduction en allemand de six pièces de théâtre anglaises, éditeur de TAGS (textes littéraires pour lycée), éditeur adjoint de TRANSFER (traduction littéraire); éditeur général de CSEL (littérature anglaise avancée de la maison d'édition Cornelsen); éditeur de REFLECTIONS (livres sur la littérature anglophone en dehors de la Grande-Bretagne et des Etats-Unis).

Auteur de livres de divers sujets. Publications récentes: *Onstage and Offstage. English Canadian Drama in Discourse* (1996*), Stimmen aus Kanada. 25 kanadische Dramen für deutsche Bühnen* (1997), *A 50th Birthday Tribute to Willy Martin Russell* (1997), *A French Window onto the Old World* (1999), (en collaboration de Nicholas Quaintmere) *A Guided Tour Through Ayckbourn Country* (1999), *Discover... First Nations Peoples in America*, livre d'étudiant et du professeur (1999/2001); *Ronald Harwood, "Taking Sides"*, édition commentée, livre d'étudiant et du professeur (1999/2000) ; *Drew Hayden Taylor, "Toronto at Dreamer's Rock"*, édition commentée, livre d'étudiant et du professeur (1995/1996), *Anne Chislett, "Flippin'In"*, édition commentée (2000). Auteur de 220 articles dans des journaux scientifiques différents, des programmes de théâtre et dans la littérature secondaire.